elvis pr

D0476558

BY JOHN ROBERTSON

Review

Copyright © 1994 Omnibus Press (A Division of Book Sales Limited)

Edited by Chris Charlesworth
Cover & Book designed by 4i Limited
Picture research by David Brolan

ISBN: 0.7119.3549.1 Order No: OP47376

Exclusive Distributors
Book Sales Limited, 8/9 Frith Street, London W1V 5TZ, UK.
Music Sales Corporation, 257 Park Avenue South, New York, NY 10010, USA.
Music Sales Pty Limited, Lisgar House, 32 Carrington Street, Sydney, Australia, NSW 2000, Australia.

To the Music Trade only:
Music Sales Limited, 8/9, Frith Street, London W1V 5TZ, UK.

Photo credits:
All photographs supplied by London Features International and Pictorial Press.

Every effort has been made to trace the copyright holders of the photographs in this book but one or two were unreachable. We would be grateful if the photographers concerned would contact us.

Printed in the United Kingdom by Ebenezer Baylis & Son Limited, Worcester.

A catalogue record for this book is available from the British Library.

OMNIBUS PRESS
LONDON · NEW YORK · SYDNEY

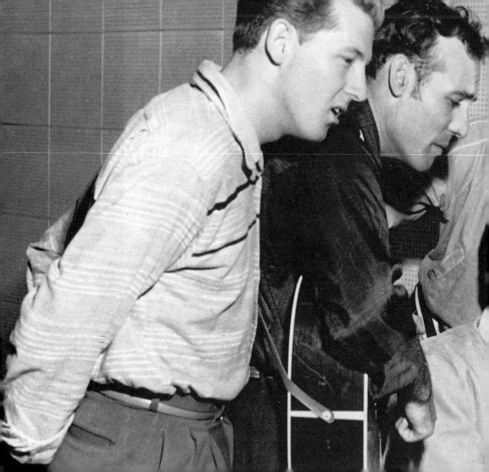

Contents

INTRODUCTION

SECTION 1 – THE SUN YEARS 1
The Sun Singles 3
The Ever Expanding Sun Collection 6
The Million Dollar Quartet 8

SECTION 2 – RCA 1956-1959 13
The RCA Singles 14
The Original Albums 1956-1959 16
The Pre-Army Films 24
Fifties Compilations 28

SECTION 3 – 1960-1968 37
The Post Army Films 39
The Singles 1960-1968 56
The Albums 1960-1968 59
The Compilations 65

SECTION 4 – THE COMEBACK 71
The Elvis TV Special 72
The Memphis Sessions 75
The Singles 77

SECTION 5 – THE FINAL YEARS 83
The Singles 84
The Studio Albums 1970-1977 86
Seventies CD Compilations 96

SECTION 6 – ELVIS LIVE 99
The Rock'n'Roll Years 100
The Concert Years 104

SECTION 7 - CD COMPILATIONS 115

Introduction

Since his death in 1977, Elvis Presley has transcended the ranks of mortal fame. The subject both of academic critiques and tabloid exposés, he's become an ever-changing 20th Century icon – an all-purpose symbol of success, excess, tragedy, irony and waste. With every year, the posthumous image of Elvis throws a deeper and darker shadow over the historical facts of his life. In death, Presley has mutated into a mythic figure, part saint, part devil, part clown.

Unlike the other legends of American popular culture, like James Dean, Marilyn Monroe and Rudolf Valentino, Elvis has survived in more than one form. Some celebrate the swaggering Fifties rocker; others the God-fearing Momma's boy, or the sleek late Sixties showman, or the bloated Vegas dinosaur. Elvis was all of these, and more; and every one of these identities can be witnessed in his music, often competing for space on the same album or song.

For all his mythical status, Elvis's music is often ignored, beyond the smattering of hits that have become common currency. This book puts that omission right, surveying his entire catalogue from his tentative outings as an 18-year-old, when he was still feeling out the potential of his talent, to the final stumbling documents of his career as a live performer, 24 years later.

The following pages offer a comprehensive guide to every aspect of Elvis's musical legacy. They are intended as a CD-buyers' guide, as increasingly that is the format in which his material is available. But large portions of Elvis's past have yet to appear on compact disc, though RCA are slowly moving towards a coherent set of retrospectives

which will assemble everything he ever recorded. Until then, this book covers all Elvis's music – whether it's readily available in every CD store, or marooned on some long-deleted LP from the Sixties.

The seven main sections of the book document different areas of Elvis's career. The first five cover his studio output chronologically – dealing with his remarkable début recordings at Sun; the internationally successful rock'n'roll he made for RCA in the Fifties; the barren years from 1960 to 1967; the unexpected comeback of 1968/69; and his tortuous decline thereafter until his early death. Additional sections chronicle his live recordings from 1955 to 1977, and finally those compilation CDs which offer an overview of his entire career.

Within each of the chronological sections, you'll find detailed critiques of his singles, original albums, movie soundtracks and relevant compilations. Together, they chronicle a long, sometimes strange journey, which carried Elvis from the musical revolution of the Fifties to the pathetic wasteland of his Hollywood movies, back to the heights with his brilliant late Sixties recordings, and then into the inexplicable despair and impotence that scarred his final years.

As you'll see, Elvis was only rarely in control of his own destiny in the two decades after he unearthed that magical blend of country music and R&B which came to be known as rock'n'roll. But even in his weakest moments, he was still one of the most remarkable pop vocalists of the century, and at his peak – whether you regard that as 1954, 1960 or 1969 – there was no-one who could match him.

Alongside a mere handful of other performers, Elvis can claim to have revolutionised the cultural history of the 20th century. He cut a hundred or more of the finest records of all time, and also produced some of the dumbest and most hilarious musical misconceptions of the rock era. It's a tangled legacy, available to the CD consumers of the Nineties on an intimidating selection of reissues and compilations. If you want to know which Elvis records to buy, what to avoid, and why, then this is the book for you.

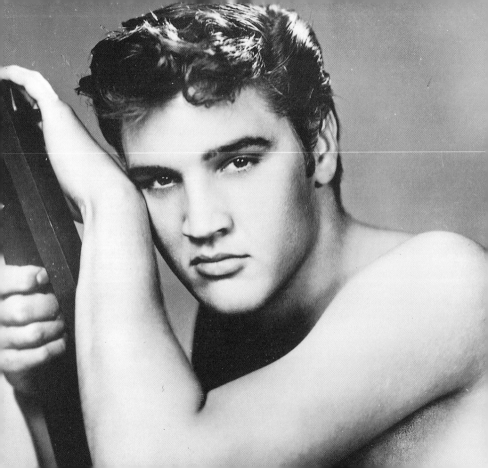

The Sun Years

1

At 706 Union Avenue, Memphis, Tennessee, stands Sun Studios – the birthplace of the most important collection of rock'n'roll tracks ever recorded. Between 1954 and 1960, Sun's owner, Sam Phillips, produced pioneering rockabilly, blues, country and pop sides by artists like Carl Perkins, Jerry Lee Lewis, Johnny Cash, Charlie Rich – and Elvis Presley.

Before Elvis was signed to Sun, in the summer of 1954, Phillips' label was renowned as a centre of excellence for the blues. Like scores of independents in the Southern states, Sun scuffled to survive from one release to the next. Phillips financed the label's early years by freelance production work, handling sessions with artists like Howlin' Wolf and B.B. King for larger companies. He supervised the making of what's generally regarded as the first rock'n'roll record, Jackie Brenston's 'Rocket 88'. He proved to be an equally sympathetic producer of hillbilly country music. And in 1954, the future King of Rock'n'Roll fell into his lap.

Elvis Presley had been born on January 8, 1935, in a tiny shack in Tupelo, Mississippi. He was raised in Memphis, and working as a truck driver for the local firm of Crown Electric when he made his first amateur recordings – at the Memphis Recording Service, part of the small Sun empire. Presley had been performing blues, country, gospel and pop songs in public for a year or two by then, and had attracted the attention of some of the hottest gospel quartets in the State. But he needed the reassurance of hearing his voice on a record, before he felt confident enough to make his music into a career.

Under the guise of cutting a record for his mother's birthday – already several months past – Elvis approached Marion Keisker, Sam Phillips' right-hand-woman, in the late summer of 1953. She captured him singing two songs, 'My Happiness' and 'That's When Your Heartaches Begin', to his own simple guitar accompaniment. The following January, he was back, cutting another pair of songs: 'Casual Love Affair' and 'I'll Never Stand In Your Way'. Impressed by the haunting melodicism of his voice, which was pitched intriguingly between a crooner's smooth slide and the low moan of the blues, Keisker kept Elvis's details on file, and reported his existence to her boss.

When Phillips needed a singer to cut a demo a few months later, he invited Presley into the studio. Their initial sessions were unproductive, but when Sam teamed Elvis with two of the label's regular sessionmen, bassist Bill Black and guitarist Scotty Moore, sparks rapidly grew into an inferno. After cutting restrained renditions of two ballads, 'Harbor Lights'

and 'I Love You Because', Presley, Moore and Black jammed around the changes of a blues song, Arthur 'Big Boy' Crudup's 'That's All Right (Mama)', while Phillips was away from the studio board. When the producer returned, he asked them what on earth they were doing – and whether they could do it again. After a handful of takes, Elvis Presley's first single was on tape, and the world of popular music was changed for ever.

Elvis issued five singles on Sun, scoring regional hits, and making brief inroads into the national country charts. He also taped around a dozen other songs during his sessions with Sam Phillips – a dozen that have survived, that is, as rumours persist of a treasure trove of missing Sun sides.

Each of his Sun singles was carefully programmed to couple a blues tune with a country song, thereby maximising the potential for sales and airplay. Before his name and face became known, no-one was sure whether Elvis was black or white – which was precisely the sound that Phillips had been looking for. Elvis's voice was part Hank Williams, part Bobby Bland, part Dean Martin, part Johnnie Ray, and part the kind of divine accident that only happens once in a century. Whether or not Sam Phillips ever voiced his much-quoted aim of finding a white man who had a "Negro sound and feel", Presley fitted the bill. Equally at home in the black or white musical traditions, he effectively moulded them into one. And his appreciation for mainstream pop music, and the tight harmonies of the top gospel quartets, enabled him to branch out way beyond the strict ghetto boundaries of blues and country. Outside, the world was waiting.

THE SUN SINGLES

THAT'S ALL RIGHT (MAMA)/BLUE MOON OF KENTUCKY (1954)

Blues purists trace a path of exploitation, of white musicians ripping off blacks, from the release of this record – which mixed a taste of hillbilly country with a Delta blues tune and produced the concoction known as rock'n'roll. Play Crudup's original alongside Presley's cover, however, and their theory implodes. Fine though Crudup's record is, it lends nothing but its basic lyrical framework to Presley's interpretation. In the hands of Elvis, Scotty and Bill, as the trio were credited on the Sun singles, 'That's All Right (Mama)' was transformed from a laboured complaint into a celebratory jubilee. Set Crudup's lugubrious vocal alongside the effortless verve of Presley's singing, and all comparisons disappear.

Presley worked similar magic on the flipside, a bluegrass tune by the father of the genre, Bill Monroe. His original had the 'high lonesome' sound of Forties bluegrass, with keening vocals and a tight, restrained rhythm. Elvis started out singing the song that way, then cut loose the chains, and played it like an uptempo blues tune. By the time the record was finished, it was hard to tell which side was country, and which was blues.

GOOD ROCKIN' TONIGHT/ I DON'T CARE IF THE SUN DON'T SHINE (1954)

The same formula was repeated on the second Sun single. 'Good Rockin' Tonight' came from a blues single by Roy Brown – an uptown, citified blues, this time, rather than the rural model Presley souped up on his début. Stopping the world in its tracks with the arrogance of his opening vocal wail, Presley set off on a roller-coaster ride across musical boundaries, calling out for everyone to recognise his power. "Tonight she'll know I'm a mighty mighty man", Presley swaggered on the middle verse, and every second of his performance matched his boast.

'I Don't Care If The Sun Don't Shine' sounded like another hillbilly song waiting for a fresh tank of gas. But it actually belonged to Tin Pan Alley, having been recorded by such sophisticates as Patti Page and Elvis's idol, Dean Martin. Elvis, Scotty and Bill turned up the tempo and played it hard and furious, and the result was every bit as dynamic as 'Blue Moon Of Kentucky'.

MILKCOW BLUES BOOGIE/YOU'RE A HEART- BREAKER (1955)

The lyrical imagery of 'Milkcow Blues Boogie' had appeared in dozens of blues (and hillbilly) songs in the decades before Elvis solidified the song for all time. It's not certain where he learned the lines – whether they came from a bluesman like Kokomo Arnold, or from the Western swing rendition of Bob Wills and his Texas Playboys. Nor is it certain whether the memorable opening seconds of his recording were contrived or improvised on the spot. Elvis, Scotty and Bill begin the song at a dirge-like tempo, before Elvis calls the band to a halt. "That don't move me," he complains. "Let's get real real gone for a change." And they do, the musicians struggling to keep pace as Elvis drives them forward with a vocal that hiccups and swoops up and down the octaves with barely contained delirium at its heart.

By complete contrast, 'You're A Heartbreaker' – actually a pop song, originally recorded by one Jimmy Heap – was presented as Presley's most sedate country performance to date. Elvis abandoned the vocal pyrotechnics of the A-side, and swung through the melody as confidently as another of his early role models, Lefty Frizzell.

I'M LEFT, YOU'RE RIGHT, SHE'S GONE/BABY LET'S PLAY HOUSE (1955)

Pitched midway between full-bore rockabilly and uptempo hillbilly, 'I'm Left, You're Right, She's Gone' was the first original song that Presley ever recorded. Written by Sun Records insider Stan Kesler, it started out as a slow blues, under the title 'My Baby's Gone' (as first heard on a legal release via 'The Complete Sun Sessions' CD).

That track was completely overshadowed by its coupling, an R&B tune based on a country hit by Eddy Arnold, and fuelled by imagery which had passed down the blues tradition for generations. Elvis launched the track with an almost inhuman series of whoops and hollers, before slicing through the lyrics with a confidence that defined the concept of 'machismo'. Mean, threatening, half sung and half sneered, 'Baby Let's Play House' encapsulated everything that was dark and enticing about the young Elvis Presley.

MYSTERY TRAIN/I FORGOT TO REMEMBER TO FORGET (1955)

Stan Kesler and self-styled rockabilly pioneer Charlie Feathers concocted the pun-filled honky-tonk ballad, 'I Forgot To Remember To Forget' – a stone country tune that Elvis sang with the flair of a Lefty Frizzell or a George Jones. Once again, though, it was the blues coupling that set the world on fire. Sam Phillips had produced Junior Parker's original version of 'Mystery Train', an eerie harbinger of doom based around the lyrical theme of a 1930s country song. For Presley's version, fellow blues fan Scotty Moore set the rhythm with a clipped, insistent guitar riff, while Elvis opened his throat and wailed, like an engineer powerless to control a ghost train heading full-tilt for a fallen bridge.

In commercial terms, this was probably the strongest of the five Sun singles; and it was certainly the most successful, topping the *Billboard* Country And Western charts towards the end of 1955. Its chart showing ensured that a major label like RCA couldn't help but be aware of Presley's potential – both as an artist and a profit-making machine.

THE EVER-EXPANDING SUN COLLECTION

When RCA purchased Elvis's contract in November 1955, they secured a case full of Elvis session tapes. As we'll see shortly, these were raided to make up the numbers on RCA's studio albums and singles between 1956 and 1959. Another Sun recording surfaced in 1965; after that, there were merely persistent rumours, until bootleg collections began appearing in the early Seventies, presenting a batch of alternate takes (including the near-legendary 'My Baby's Gone', the bluesier role model for 'I'm Left, You're Right, She's Gone').

For anyone who didn't have access to the original, mono singles, the Sun recordings were available only in ludicrous fake stereo from the early Sixties through to 1975, when RCA finally released their first Sun-centred Presley album. There have been several subsequent attempts at the same operation, but still hardcore Presley-philes maintain that there is a secret vault filled with previously unheard Sun masters. That there may be; but it's near certain RCA don't have access to it, or else those tracks would surely have been released by now.

The late Seventies and Eighties also saw the legal (or semi-legal, in some cases) release of other material long rumoured to have survived – live recordings of Elvis, Scotty Moore and Bill Black taped during the Sun era, plus the fabled 'Million Dollar Quartet' tape, recorded at Sun a year after Elvis left for RCA.

THE ELVIS PRESLEY SUN COLLECTION (1975)

It took British Presley fans – notably the *NME* journalist Roy Carr – to force RCA into compiling a long-overdue album of what seemed, at the time, like the complete Sun recordings. With the exception of an alternate take of 'I Love You Because', issued on 1974's 'A Legendary Performer' LP, everything on the original pressing of this album had been issued in the Fifties. But here it was on sale in one budget-priced package, and without the distorted, artificial remixing of previous reissues. It was also the first Presley LP to include lengthy, informative, factual sleeve notes.

A few months after this LP appeared, RCA 'discovered' a previously unknown Sun out-take: a cover of the crooner's favourite, 'Harbor Lights'. This was added to the subsequent pressings of the 'Sun Collection', only for the process to be repeated. This time the addition to the canon was 'When It Rains, It Really Pours', a 1955 prototype for the recording included on 1965's 'Elvis For Everyone' LP. That surfaced on 'A Legendary Performer Vol. 4' in 1983. Next to be uncovered was the undubbed recording of 'Tomorrow Night', which had first surfaced with additional instrumentation on that same 1965 LP. Stripped of its later ornamentation, it appeared on the 1985

collection, 'Reconsider Baby'.

A few months earlier, the boxed album set 'A Golden Celebration' had offered an entire suite of Sun out-takes. Among them was the legendary 'My Baby's Gone', so titled by bootleggers in the early Seventies, but actually an early, bluesy arrangement of 'I'm Left, You're Right, She's Gone'; a pure country fragment of 'Blue Moon Of Kentucky'; an equally brief 'I'll Never Let You Go'; alternate versions of 'Harbor Lights', 'That's All Right' and 'I Don't Care If The Sun Don't Shine'; and that magical 'When It Rains, It Really Pours'.

When RCA announced they now had access to more than a dozen alternate takes from the Sun years, it was obviously time for a complete revamp.

THE COMPLETE SUN SESSIONS (1987)

To a chorus of praise from most sides, blurred only slightly by howls of disgust by perfectionists, 'The Complete Sun Sessions' gave these seminal recordings their most prestigious setting to date. The lengthy notes by Presley biographer Peter Guralnick set the scene and cast aside some myths, while the two-LP set itself gathered up every Sun track released to date, and added nine further out-takes.

These weren't quite as thrilling as they might have been, as they comprised three additional takes of 'I Love You Because' and six of 'I'm Left, You're Right, She's Gone'. Confirmation of their existence suggested to the detractors that RCA must be sitting on similar treasure troves for other songs in their archive – a theory for which the release of 'The Complete Fifties Masters' in 1992 added more evidence (see Section B).

Sadly, this was one release where the vinyl edition outstripped the CD. Two full LPs contained too much music for one 5" disc, so six tracks were dropped to prevent the need for a two-CD set: takes 1 and 4 of 'I Love You Because' and takes 8, 10, 11 and 12 of 'I'm Left, You're Right, She's Gone'. At least RCA had the honesty to drop the 'Complete' from the title of the CD.

THE MILLION DOLLAR QUARTET

Myth or hype? The jury's still out on that question. But in theNineties, at least we have some of the evidence in our hands.

On December 4, 1956, international star Elvis Presley returned to Sun Studios, little more than a year after he'd left the company for RCA. He arrived as Carl Perkins, the man who'd written 'Blue Suede Shoes' and assumed the mantle of Sun's top rock artist after Presley's departure, was recording his new single, 'Matchbox'. On piano was one of Sun's newest signings, Jerry Lee Lewis. On drums and bass were Perkins' regular sidemen, W.S. Holland and Clayton Perkins. And sitting out in the control room was fellow Sun artist, Johnny Cash.

After the session was over, Elvis headed for the piano and began to sing 'Blueberry Hill'. As Cash, Perkins and Lewis gathered round him, Sam Phillips called a local news photographer, who high-tailed it to the studio, and took a photo of the three established performers alongside Lewis, the man whom Phillips thought was headed for equal success.

The *Memphis Press-Scimitar* ran the photo alongside a story about the session; a few days later, Phillips mailed the picture to DJs, alongside a copy of the press story and a brief note of his own.

As Lewis followed Perkins, Cash and Presley into the ranks of stardom, the legend of that afternoon grew. Someone coined the title of 'Million Dollar Quartet' for the session; and as the years went by, speculation grew about the existence of a tape, and its likely contents.

Confirmation of the first issue came in 1977, when Sun's new owner, Shelby Singleton, announced the imminent release of five albums documenting the session. RCA followed through with a court injunction, and the album never appeared. The inevitable happened, and in 1980, a bootleg was released with around 30 minutes of the tape intact. Charly Records in Europe, who handled the Sun catalogue there, followed through with a 'legal' release. Ownership of the tapes was still open to question, of course, while many observers were

amused to find 11 of the 22 'tracks' on the album credited "Trad Arr. H Young", with the copyright residing in Charly's own publishing subsidiary.

But Charly did at least get the 'Quartet' tapes out of the closet, and achieved a further breakthrough in 1987 by extending the album to a two-LP set. RCA matched it with an 'official' release, though without the word 'Complete' that Charly had used in their title. They obviously knew something Charly didn't: when 'The Complete Fifties Masters' appeared in 1992, a Million Dollar Quartet out-take of 'Reconsider Baby' was included. Its 'discovery' begs the question of what other tapes RCA have secreted in their vaults.

And the music? Well, it wasn't the full-bore quartet album that fans had been hoping for. Johnny Cash was conspicuous by his absence, having gone shopping before Sam Phillips turned the tape recorder on. And the remaining trio of Presley, Lewis and Perkins – supported by Carl's band – were simply jamming, rather than pursuing worked-out arrangements. But with those qualifications, what remained was history – ephemeral, perhaps, but history all the same. Beginning with a clutch of country gospel tunes, the Million Dollar Trio soon drifted towards pop and rock'n'roll, expressing their shared admiration for Chuck Berry's

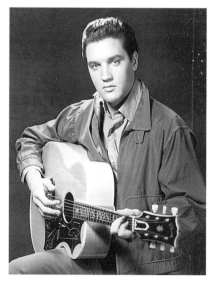

'Brown Eyed Handsome Man'. Elvis revealed that Pat Boone's hit 'Don't Forbid Me' had first been offered to him; reported excitedly on Jackie Wilson's impression of his own singing style at a show he'd seen by Billy Ward's Dominoes; and débuted 'Is It So Strange'. Carl Perkins offered enthusiastic rockabilly guitar, and essayed some tentative vocal leads on a couple of country tunes. And Jerry Lee, with all the carefree confidence of youthful genius, matched Elvis lick-for-lick, hijacking the gospel songs, and ending the session by running through both sides of his recently recorded début single. None of this material could possibly have been issued at the time: nearly 40 years later, the unedited tapes transport us back to a time when Presley, Perkins and Lewis were precocious young men, thrilled as much by their musical potential as by the early lure of fame.

RCA
1956-1959

Under stiff competition from leading R&B independent Atlantic Records, RCA Victor signed Elvis Presley to an exclusive recording contract on November 20, 1955. Their final offer to Colonel Parker was a mere $40,000 – which included $5,000 as a personal advance to Elvis (he promptly blew the stash on a Cadillac for his beloved mother), and $15,000 to cover the purchase of Presley's music publishing firm.

Included in the deal, which effectively saved Sam Phillips' Sun label from going to the wall, was access to, and ownership of, all Presley's Sun recordings, issued and otherwise. In retrospect, Sam Phillips made one of the biggest mistakes of his life in agreeing to those terms: seven unreleased Sun tracks surfaced on RCA during the next decade, while RCA were also able to reissue all the original Sun singles. By buying out Phillips' entire Presley archive, they pre-empted an ugly sales war between his first RCA recordings and re-promotions of his first five 45s by Sun. Unlike Sun, with its heritage of hillbilly and blues, or Atlantic, with its deep reservoir of R&B talent, RCA was a pop label, pure and simple. A&R man Steve Sholes handed Presley over to producer/guitarist Chet Atkins with one instruction: to make hit records, that would extend beyond the specialist regional charts to the *Billboard* national Hot 100, and then around the world.

The measure of RCA's success is obvious from any book of chart statistics, in Britain or America. Within a year of his first release on the label, Elvis Presley was not only RCA's most successful artist, but also the best-selling singer in the world. The unchallenged king of rock'n'roll, he was also channelled into creating a series of ballad hits that immediately diversified his market. He was encouraged to record albums, and to make movies. He was aided in Colonel Tom Parker's quest to get Elvis on every important variety TV show in America. And he was groomed for stardom with such commanding persistence that his call-up into the US Forces in 1958 became headline news around the world.

Did RCA stifle or even smother the Hillbilly Cat who had invented rockabilly music in Sun's Memphis studios? The purists would argue yes, pointing to the immediate smoothing-over of his natural rawness and vocal attack, and the gradual encroachment of pop music values onto a sound that had once threatened to rend the fabric of Fifties pop asunder. RCA's defenders, meanwhile, would claim that by forcing Elvis to tailor his rockin' energy for the mass market, they transformed him from a two-year wonder into a superstar for life. Had he remained at Sun, they contend, his career would have burnt out

after at most a dozen local hits, and some other contender would have upset the cosy conservatism of the American entertainment business.

The reality is that RCA, with the hands-on aid of Colonel Tom Parker, both made and killed Elvis. After setting him loose on the world, they gradually hauled in the reins: a decade after signing to RCA, Elvis was the world's most famous entertainer, and at the same time completely washed up as a creative force. When he signed on the dotted line in November 1955, he wanted success first and foremost. That he achieved, only to discover the clichéd truth that success means nothing without fulfilment. Having relished the pure self-expression of his Sun recordings, Elvis could measure every painful inch of his decline after he returned from the Army in 1960.

THE RCA SINGLES 1956-1959

Ten days before he signed with RCA, Elvis was visited in his Nashville hotel room, during a DJ convention, by songwriter Mae Axton, who played him a simple demo sung by Glen Reeves. The song on the tape, co-written by Axton and Tommy Durden, was a slow, anguished blues tune called 'Heartbreak Hotel'. Elvis immediately recognised its potential, and promised Axton he'd record it.

Two months later, at RCA's studio in the same city, Elvis warmed up with Ray Charles' 'I Got A Woman', which he'd been playing on the road for several months, and then kept to his word. 'Heartbreak Hotel' duly became his first RCA single, and an international hit. It was startlingly different from anything he'd cut at Sun, and also far removed from the carefree swagger of the archetypal rock'n'roller. On his first major-label release, Elvis seemed to realise that there was more at stake than simply a hit record.

Although his regular sidekicks, Scotty Moore and Bill Black, played on his sessions throughout the Fifties, and Moore for almost a decade after that, there was a distinct shift of sound on the RCA recordings. Steve Sholes and Chet Atkins augmented the simple trio with several extra musicians – notably drummer D.J. Fontana, plus Atkins himself on additional guitar and a keyboard player (often Floyd Cramer). More importantly, he recruited the popular gospel group, The Jordanaires, to provide vocal support. Varying between bluesy doo-wop and straight-laced barbershop quartet singing, The Jordanaires offered consistently tasteful backing for Presley's remarkable vocal range, but inevitably softened the raunchiness that had been so apparent on the Sun sides.

RCA's staff also encouraged Presley to record pop tunes with vaguely country or blues overtones, rather than songs that belonged firmly in either camp. Often, as on 'I Was The One', the flipside of 'Heartbreak Hotel', Elvis veered towards self-parody, hiccupping and scatting his way through a banal lyric with a playful air that suggested rebellion might soon be on the cards. But as one upbeat pop song succeeded another, the hint of rebellion ebbed away.

Ignoring the reissues of Sun recordings, Elvis's early RCA singles plot a steady course away from the cutting edge.

'I Want You, I Need You, I Love You' was 'I Was The One' writ larger; the blues power of 'Hound Dog' was undercut by the semi-satirical pop of 'Don't Be Cruel'; 'Too Much', 'All Shook Up' and 'Teddy Bear' accentuated the softening of his style; and 'Love Me Tender' injected stark romantic balladry into the equation.

Not that Elvis's singing was ever less than brilliant, however; and sometimes, as with the discordant clang of metallic guitar that launched Scotty Moore's second solo on 'Hound Dog', or The Jordanaires' energetic back-up on 'Teddy Bear', his support crew kept pace. But revolution was quickly being turned into pastiche.

From the end of 1957 onwards, there was a heartening move towards raw rock'n'roll, with the rasping vocals of 'Jailhouse Rock', 'Hard Headed Woman' and 'One Night' – a savage blues song which was admittedly toned down from his world-weary original for Elvis's reading, but still demonstrated that the man remembered how to *live* a song. Elsewhere, though, on 'I Beg Of You' and

'Wear My Ring Around Your Neck', parody was setting in. It took a revamped country song, 'A Fool Such As I' in 1958, to prove that Elvis could combine blues, country, pop, rock'n'roll, satire, conviction and joyous enthusiasm in one neat three-minute package. And on even the weakest of the Fifties singles, there's the glory of that voice – apparently limitless in its potential, and effortlessly transcending the most banal material.

THE ORIGINAL ALBUMS 1956-1959

ELVIS PRESLEY (1956)

Commonly known as 'Rock'n'Roll' (though the UK LP of that title has a different track listing), the artwork of Elvis's first album incorporates one of the most familiar images in rock iconography. The LP's graphics even inspired a tribute from The Clash, who borrowed the design for their 'London Calling' set in 1979.

With just one Elvis single in the shops, RCA were able to capitalise on their purchase of the Sun Records tapes in preparing this album in February 1956. Nothing on the LP had been issued before, and with most potential purchasers having heard nothing more of Presley than 'Heartbreak Hotel' and 'I Was The One', 'Elvis Presley' provided an instant introduction to the singer's poise and range.

Of the five Sun-era recordings included on the album, only one – the jumping 'Just Because' – qualified as rockabilly. The rest highlighted Elvis's early infatuation with singing ballads, something that Sam Phillips hadn't wanted to expose on the Sun singles. 'I Love You Because' was already a country standard, but 'Blue Moon' stepped back a further generation to the 1930s. Elvis's rendition was steeped in echo, with a vocal that almost defined the word 'ghostly', and a curious percussion motif running eerily through the track. 'I'll Never Let You Go' was equally atmospheric.

But the jewel among these Sun leftovers was the blues ballad 'Trying To Get To You' – sung with all the vocal dramatics of 'Baby Let's Play House', plus an additional dose of passion. Almost savage in its naked emotion, it easily outshone everything else on the LP.

The seven RCA recordings were marginally slicker, and had fuller instrumentation. But they certainly weren't close to being tame. 'I'm Counting On You' reproduced the unsettling balladry of 'I'll Never Let You Go', while 'Money Honey' remade The Drifters' 1954 hit in Presley's image. The rocker stole the honours, however, from the vibed-up dart through Carl Perkins' 'Blue Suede Shoes' to the super-charged demolition of Ray Charles' 'I Got A Woman'. Best of all – partly because it was so obviously contrived – was the ridiculous 'One Sided Love Affair', in which Presley disembowelled a piece of romantic fluff, one minute moaning with sexual menace, the next hiccuping like a clown, before sneering down his nose at the entire endeavour on the final chorus. It was a towering performance, arrogant and utterly in control – a description that could just as easily be applied to the entire album.

The US line-up of the album is available on CD – credited as "digitally remastered", but suffering from an excess of hiss and distortion. For the brilliance of the music, that is still a price worth paying.

ELVIS (1956)

Fortunately for all concerned, more imagination went into the recording of this record than its title. For the second time in a year, Elvis demonstrated his unique ability to cover any base you had in mind, and several more you never thought of. 'Rip It Up', 'Ready Teddy' and 'Long Tall Sally' presented a triple threat to Little Richard's belief that he was the king of rock'n'roll; 'Paralyzed' performed the same feat on an original song; 'So Glad You're Mine' completed a trio of dazzling Arthur Crudup covers (after 1954's 'That's All Right' and 'My Baby Left Me' earlier in 1956); and 'Love Me' proved that Elvis knew the power of his sexual image.

In the midst of all this bluster and potency came a rare early glimpse of Elvis's sentimental side. The tearjerker ballad 'Old

Shep' was a country standard, creating enormous dollops of fake emotion out of the death of a child's beloved dog. Elvis had first sung this maudlin piece in public at the age of 10; now, 11 years later, he invested it with all the anguish at his command, creating a kitsch masterpiece that had nothing to do with rock'n'roll, and everything to do with his complex emotional make-up.

Available on CD, again with the problems you'd expect when working from un-remastered Fifties tapes.

ELVIS' CHRISTMAS ALBUM (1957)

The seasonal tie-in has been a hardy staple of the music business ever since they invented the gramophone record. But Elvis's Christmas offering for 1957 proved to be one of the most controversial. His rendition of 'O Little Town Of Bethlehem', was appropriately respectful, but many critics were disgusted by his only slightly less reverent reading of 'Silent Night'. Worse still, he dared to toy with a song so tied to the showbusiness

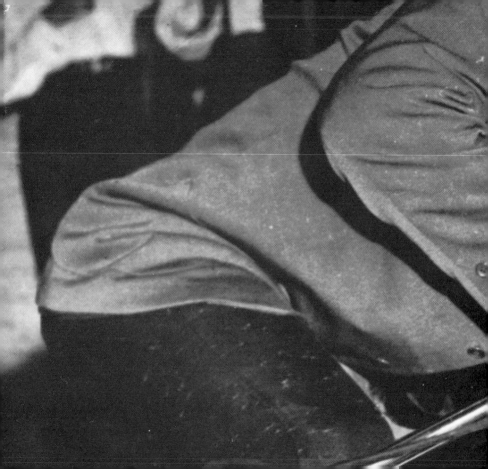

conception of the festive season that it had taken on almost religious significance – the Bing Crosby hit, 'White Christmas'. Presley added a slice of jazz flavour to the arrangement, and scatted his way through a couple of choruses as if he was lazing in the sun on Malibu Beach. Such was the outrage that many US radio stations barred their DJs from airing such an iconoclastic performance.

When Elvis turned from Jesus and Bing to saints, in the person of Santa Claus, no-one batted an eye. Jerry Leiber and Mike Stoller threw together a raw blues tune called 'Santa Claus Is Back In Town', which Elvis treated like gutbucket R&B. The more lighthearted 'Santa Bring My Baby Back To Me' was closer to the breezy air of 'Teddy Bear', while 'Here Comes Santa Claus' was pure pop. Aside from the Leiber/Stoller offering, the real gem was 'Blue Christmas', a smoochy ballad with an appropriate blues feel, which belatedly became a mid-Sixties hit single in Britain.

Besides the eight seasonal songs, RCA threw in four gospel recordings Elvis had issued as an EP earlier in 1957. His first dabblings with the genre in the studio, they went some way towards defusing the bad press Elvis had attracted for the sexuality of his stage shows, without upsetting his hardcore fans. 'I Believe' had recently been a major hit for Frankie Laine, while 'Peace In The Valley', 'It Is No Secret' and 'Take My Hand Precious Lord' featured in the repertoire of most gospel performers. Elvis was supported by The Jordanaires on these heartfelt recordings, which were carried off with a hint of insincerity.

Surprisingly good sound on the CD release of this album – plus the bonus of some brief studio chatter leading into "Blue Christmas".

FOR LP FANS ONLY (1959)

As its title suggested, this album was a holding manoeuvre on RCA's part. Elvis had been in the US Army for almost a year when it appeared, the label was about to unveil their last 'new' single, and there was another year to do until he was demobbed. They needed Elvis material in the shops, and so 1958 and 1959 saw a constant stream of reissues and repackages. Besides the two 'Golden Records' collections mentioned elsewhere, the 'Christmas Album' was reissued in 1958, various EPs were concocted out of previously issued songs, and there was even an extended-play release called 'Elvis Sails', made up of interview material taped as Presley departed for West Germany.

With the differing configurations and track listings issued around the world, 'For LP Fans Only' and its follow-up, 'A Date With Elvis', carried slightly different contents in different areas of the globe. The original American release threw together some Sun singles, a couple of RCA B-sides, and some 1956 recordings only made available in the US on EPs. These included a fiery cover of the Joe Turner/Bill Haley hit, 'Shake, Rattle And Roll', a rockabilly romp through Arthur Crudup's 'My Baby Left Me', and the definitive rendition of Lloyd Price's New Orleans blues standard, 'Lawdy Miss Clawdy'. When you added in proto-rocka-

billy classics like 'That's All Right', 'Mystery Train' and 'You're A Heartbreaker', no LP fans could complain of being shortchanged.

The US CD of 'For LP Fans Only' has 10 tracks; the UK equivalent features 14, and improved (though by no means perfect) sound quality.

A DATE WITH ELVIS (1959)

Working on the assumption that a date with Elvis was what every female fan desired, RCA compiled a second makeweight collection to while away the hours until their commercial saviour returned. This was very much the mixture as before: the Sun singles this time included 'Blue Moon Of Kentucky', 'Milkcow Blues Boogie', 'Baby Let's Play House' and 'Good Rockin' Tonight', all making their first appearance on album; while RCA also added in three of the EP-only tracks from the 'Jailhouse Rock' soundtrack. Strangely, they managed to omit 'Don't Leave Me Now', which didn't surface on any Elvis LP during his lifetime. Another bonus was the intense ballad 'Is

It So Strange', which provoked one of Elvis's finest vocal performances of the decade. Moody, mysterious and low-key, it easily lived up to the promise of its title.

Another case where the UK CD follows the original 14-track UK line-up of the album, rather than the shorter US listing.

THE PRE-ARMY FILMS

Just eleven weeks after Elvis's first RCA recording session, he took his first screen test, at Paramount Films' lot in Hollywood. For Colonel Parker, a movie career was an obvious way of expanding his charge's showbusiness potential. For Elvis himself, it was a novelty and a thrill to add to the plethora of new experiences that his major-label contract had already brought. And for Hollywood, Elvis represented the youth market – an opportunity for Paramount to reach the audience who had responded to the youthful angst and surly rebelliousness of James Dean and Marlon Brando. If Elvis could act, then he could be coached as a teen matinée idol, in the knowledge that his musical success would provide free

advertising for any film he made.

Early in April 1956, Paramount affixed Presley's name to a three-film, seven-year exclusive deal. In the event, the liaison lasted for five films, but only four years – during which time Elvis gave his only acting performances worthy of the title. Beginning in *Love Me Tender* as a minor player in a period Western, Presley quickly graduated to top-billing for the semi-biographical *Loving You*. In his next two films, the clichéd but vibrant *Jailhouse Rock* and the feisty *King Creole*, Elvis was forced to act, rather than simply provide an amiable version of his own personality. Only at the beginning and end of the Sixties did such a chance arise again. No wonder, then, that film buffs have little time for his increasingly formulaic movie-work after 1960.

The first four Presley pictures established a tradition, with a title song that was invariably issued as a single, and sufficient musical distraction on the soundtrack to fill an EP, or later an LP, with new Elvis recordings. Having begun his RCA recording career in Nashville and New

York, Elvis's sessions in the late Fifties were invariably re-sited in Hollywood, where he could tape one set of performances in front of the movie cameras, and then another in the perfectionist environment of the recording studios.

LOVE ME TENDER (1956)

Third in the billing, beneath established stars Richard Egan and Debra Paget, Elvis Presley was no doubt supposed to regard his movie début as part of a gentle learning process, *en route* to a lengthy career as an entertainer. Twentieth-Century Fox's attitude towards their young protégé was summed up by their choice of vehicle: Elvis's character was shot dead midway through the proceedings, and only reappeared late in the movie as a ghost. Indeed, the film was supposed to be called *The Reno Brothers*: only as shooting began in August 1956 did the studio realise that they could capitalise on a hit single by naming the film after a song. 'Love Me Tender' was duly released in September, and topped the charts in October – per-

fect preparation for the première in November.

Rock'n'roll was scratched from the agenda for the four soundtrack songs – partly, no doubt, because the movie was set in the pre-rock era of 1865. The songs were recorded with male vocal accompaniment, but the minimum of instrumentation; and setting the precedent for the future, the film and record versions of the title track were noticeably different. The four songs were issued as an EP to tie in with the première.

All four of the film songs, plus an out-take of the title track, appear on 'Essential Elvis'.

LOVING YOU (1957)

Learning from their under-estimation of Presley's popularity first time around, Fox made sure that their star survived to the end of the script in *Loving You*. Suitably enough, Elvis played a fame-bound hillbilly singer, which allowed for plenty of performance scenes on camera. Rock'n'roll was perfectly in keeping with the development of the plot, so Elvis was able to return briefly to the rockabilly style of his Sun recordings for songs like '(Let's Have A) Party' and 'Got A Lot O'Livin' To Do', besides recording the first version of 'Mean Woman Blues', which soon became a rock standard. 'Teddy Bear' and 'Hot Dog' provided the pop input, while only the sentimental title song – a blatant recasting of Elvis's first movie theme – and 'Lonesome Cowboy' threatened the uptempo mood.

Spreading the seven film songs across two EPs (with the bonus of the ballad 'True Love'), RCA also issued Elvis's first soundtrack album, expanded to full length in the States with extra studio cuts like 'Blueberry Hill' and 'Have I Told You Lately That I Love You'. In Britain, the 'Loving You' LP began life as a short but sweet 10" album, a mere eight songs long, and was then expanded by adding the four tunes from the gospel EP 'Peace In The Valley'.

The original British CD release of the extended 12-track line-up was a disaster. Listed as "Digital Stereo" on the spine, it sounded as if the engineer had spread his lunch across the recording tape before mastering the set. A subsequent revamp was only marginally better. Almost all the film songs were included on 'Essential Elvis Vol. 1', plus alternate takes; all of them, of course, appear on 'The Complete Fifties Masters'.

JAILHOUSE ROCK (1957)

Elia Kazan's brilliant 1957 movie, *A Face In The Crowd*, dissected and destroyed the very myth – of a hillbilly hayseed turned national star – which had powered *Loving You*. So it was no coincidence that a little of Kazan's cynicism entered *Jailhouse Rock*, which saw Elvis playing an ex-con who achieves fame at the expense of his prison buddy and mentor.

Despite its occasional lapses into melodrama, *Jailhouse Rock* remains one of the two finest Presley movies – not least for its brilliant set-piece accompanying the title track, in which all vestiges of realism are scattered to the winds, and pure expressionism takes over.

A scorching, blues-based rocker from the fertile minds of Jerry Leiber and Mike

Stoller, 'Jailhouse Rock' itself was as powerful as anything Elvis recorded at RCA in the Fifties. Of the remaining songs, 'Treat Me Nice' returned to the feel of soft-rockers like 'Teddy Bear', while 'Young And Beautiful' was the token ballad. If '(You're So Square) Baby I Don't Care' reeked of artificiality, nothing could stand in the way of 'I Want To Be Free' – an overwrought, clichéd blues ballad which Elvis twisted into a statement of pure passion.

Six songs were included in the movie, in all: apart from 'Treat Me Nice', relegated to the flipside of the title song, they were all contained on the 'Jailhouse Rock' soundtrack EP.

Check 'Essential Elvis' for out-takes; otherwise listen to 'The Complete Fifties Masters'.

KING CREOLE (1958)

If one Elvis movie deserves to survive the century, it's *King Creole* – the film which brought the second era of his career to a close. Paramount Films had to beg for Elvis's draft to be deferred so he could make the picture: apart from one mid-service recording session in June 1958, it was his last gasp of freedom before he began his military service.

Based on the kind of popular literary success that always translates well to the screen – Harold Robbins' novel, *A Stone For Danny Fisher* – *King Creole* had dramatic strengths that went beyond its status as a Presley movie. It also boasted the richest soundtrack of any Elvis film, spawning a spin-off LP that perhaps lacked the rootsy musicianship of his Sun sides, but offered a startling vocal confidence in its place.

As yet untamed by his stint in the Army, Elvis attacked the *King Creole* songs with a swaggering cockiness and full-throated power. The New Orleans locations encouraged the use of Dixieland orchestrations, which merely heightened the excitement of 'Hard Headed Woman' and 'Dixieland Rock'. But it was 'Trouble' – a semi-satirical piece of R&B *braggadocio* – which captured all Elvis's pre-Army glory. Ten years later, he returned to the song in his NBC TV special, when his entire career was on the line.

Missing from the film, and the album, was 'Danny', a song which surfaced only after Elvis's death. Retitled 'Lonely Blue Boy', it became a 1959 hit for one of the stars to emerge during Elvis's Army stint, Conway Twitty.

Early pressings of this album on CD had lousy, fake stereo sound; RCA's second attempt substituted straightforward mono hiss. Stick with the 'Fifties Masters' box set instead – or the original vinyl. For out-takes listen to 'Essential Elvis Volume 3'.

FIFTIES COMPILATIONS

ELVIS' GOLDEN RECORDS (1958)

Deservedly titled, this was the first of four such volumes issued over the next decade. Every song but one had been culled from a million-selling single – the exception being the stage favourite 'Love Me', picked from Presley's second LP, 'Elvis'.

The UK CD release of 'Golden Records' uses the original US track listing.

50,000,000 ELVIS FANS CAN'T BE WRONG (ELVIS' GOLDEN RECORDS VOLUME 2) (1959)

Purely functional, but a vital artefact for its glorious cover showing the soon-to-be-King in his gold lamé suit, '50,000,000 Fans' collected together the A- and B-sides of five of his six 1958 and 1959 singles. The missing coupling was 'Hard Headed Woman'/'Don't Ask Me Why', for the simple reason that both songs were already included on the 'King Creole' LP.

The CD has neither the original 10-track US line-up, or the 14-track version issued in Britain at the same time, but a revised 14-song selection midway between the two.

ROCKER (1985)

Wonderful music, and concept, but lousy value for money: a mere 12 tracks were included on this CD release. The fact that they all came from 1956 and 1957, and matched the title of the album, wasn't much compensation.

You'll find more vintage Elvis rockers, in better sound quality, elsewhere.

THE ELVIS PRESLEY COLLECTION VOLUME 1 (1986)

The first of four CD-only sets that collected familiar Elvis hits from 1954 to 1971, this 16-track compilation offered a token Sun recording, 'That's All Right', before skipping through a fairly obvious selection of RCA material from 1956 to 1957.

The best quality CD presentation of the initial Presley hits — at least until it was superseded by the 'Fifties Masters' box.

THE ELVIS PRESLEY COLLECTION VOLUME 2 (1986)

The second in the series kicked off with 'Teddy Bear' from 1957 and ended in 1960, with the first three singles Elvis issued after his return from the Services.

As above: excellent sound and certainly far better than the two 'Golden Records' releases.

ESSENTIAL ELVIS (1986)

The two 'Collection' volumes listed above were compiled and prepared for release in Britain, where Roger Semon had grown tired of seeing sub-standard US compilations littering the shelves. They were simply a dry run for two remarkably ambitious series of Presley retrospectives – a run of single albums bearing the apt title 'Essential', and then a procession of box sets that began tentatively with 'Collector's Gold', but matured to perfection with 'The Complete Fifties Masters' and 'From Nashville To Memphis'.

The first 'Essential Elvis' was the least ambitious of the three, but its mere existence astounded Presley fans. For the first time, someone in authority had realised that there was enormous interest in Elvis's studio out-takes – and not just from the barren Sixties, the source for several tracks on 1980's 'Elvis Aron Presley' boxed set (not available on CD). What's more, 'Essential Elvis' had a theme that didn't involve Christmas, children or Valentine's Day. Roger Semon set out to prepare the definitive musical portrait of Presley's first three movies, *Love Me Tender*, *Loving You* and *Jailhouse Rock*. At this point, there were no out-takes available from the début, so Semon contented himself with the over-arranged version of the title song that originally ran over the end credits.

But from *Loving You* and *Jailhouse Rock*, a host of alternate takes and rarities was uncovered. They included four 'new' versions of 'Loving You', two in the familiar ballad style, two arranged as a blues; the 'live' takes of 'Mean Woman Blues' and 'Jailhouse Rock' heard in the movies; and alternate takes of 'Party', 'Got A Lot O' Livin' To Do', 'Treat Me Nice', 'Young And Beautiful', 'Baby I Don't Care', 'I Want To Be Free' and 'Don't Leave Me Now'. These out-takes didn't differ much from the released versions, but that didn't worry the fans one iota.

The CD release of this album includes four tracks not included on the LP.

STEREO '57 (ESSENTIAL ELVIS VOLUME 2) (1988)

'Elvis Goofs Off' might have been a more accurate title of this amusingly revelatory set, which concentrated on a single batch of sessions from mid-January 1957. They produced the 'Peace In The Valley' spiritual EP, the 'All Shook Up' single and a variety of LP tracks – and were recorded 'binaurally', the direct forerunner of two-track stereo. This allowed studio wizard 'Boppin' Bob Jones to mix the entire album into stereo – our earliest chance to hear Elvis this way.

That was simply the icing: the vast majority of the album was also previously unreleased. Aside from Elvis regularly corpsing with laughter as he attempted to sing without being distracted by the rest of the band, this allowed the world to hear his original version of 'I Beg Of You' (re-cut for a single a few months later) for the first time. There were four takes of that song to relish, but another dozen or so of 'Blueberry Hill' (note Elvis trying his damnedest to sound like Fats Domino), 'That's When Your Heartaches Begin' and 'Peace In The Valley'. The highlight was a delicious reading of 'Is It So Strange', where Elvis soared unexpectedly into falsetto for one of the final lines. Students of the Peter Sellers style of acting could enjoy the frequently hysterical breakdowns, meanwhile, which proved that the infamous 'laughing version' of 'Are You Lonesome Tonight' wasn't a drug-crazed aberration.

Once again, the CD release runs four tracks longer than the vinyl version.

ESSENTIAL ELVIS VOLUME 3: HITS LIKE NEVER BEFORE (1990)

Frequently overlooked by rock'n'roll purists who insist Elvis passed his prime in 1956, his 1958 sessions (the last before he joined the Army) produced some of the most succulent, thrilling music of his career. To prove the point, the third of the 'Essential' albums unveiled another batch of perfect quality out-takes – all but a handful previously unreleased. In January, February and June 1958, Elvis cut the soundtrack for *King Creole*, then recorded the singles that would keep his name in the public eye while he was in the Services. The film supplies an alternate take or two of the title track – including a bizarre Scotty Moore guitar solo on take 18 – plus the

full-length duet version of 'Crawfish' heard in the movie, the 'Main Title Theme' and much more besides.

But the two singles sessions provide the real goods here. There are several stabs at the contrived but amusing 'I Got Stung', one of which dissolves into an unexpected version of 'When Irish Eyes Are Smiling'. 'Wear My Ring Around Your Neck' is heard before and after Elvis himself added some instrumental overdubs, boogieing at the piano and then slapping the back of his guitar for percussion. Take 1 of 'A Big Hunk O' Love' rushes by in a chaotic frenzy, but the highlight is 'Ain't That Loving You Baby', cut at this 1958 session but unaccountably not issued in any form until 1964. Three out-takes here not only confirm the song as one of the best blues in Elvis's repertoire, but also catch his instruction to his guitarist/producer, Chet Atkins: "Boogie, Chet". That advice must have sounded revolutionary to the man who invented the laid-back, soporific 'Nashville Sound'.

As usual, there are four bonus cuts on the CD edition.

THE COMPLETE FIFTIES MASTERS (1992)

Justly nominated for a Grammy Award as the year's best reissue package, 'The Complete Fifties Masters' set out to stake Elvis Presley's definitive claim to be the King of Rock'n'Roll – and to cement that reputation for eternity. Across five CDs, it charted the magnificent music that Presley recorded between 1953 and 1958, ending with a disc of rarities that introduced several vital pieces to the jigsaw of his early career.

Note the title of this set, incidentally: 'Complete Masters' rather than 'Complete Recordings'. Compilers Roger Semon and Ernst Jorgenson didn't attempt to assemble all the alternate takes that had been issued on the 'Essential' albums. Instead, they concentrated on gathering together the 'master' recording of every song in Elvis's Fifties catalogue. For the purposes of this set, that catalogue stretched as far back as 1953, when the 18-year-old Elvis recorded 'My Happiness' and 'That's When Your Heartaches Begin' on a scratchy acetate at Sun Studios. Those performances have nothing to do with rock'n'roll, but they display the same ghostly, ethereal presence as Sun sides like 'Blue Moon', while Elvis toys with a variety of vocal *personae* – one moment crooning like Bing Crosby, the next playing with syllables like Johnnie Ray, or showing off the melisma of the gospel soloists. As a clue to his musical breeding-ground, both these songs came from the vocal group tradition – 'Happiness' from The Pied Pipers, among others, and 'Heartaches' from The Ink Spots – and Elvis treated them like holy writ.

From there, it's a parade of jewels through the Sun years, the initial flurry of rock'n'roll at RCA, the early films, and finally the commanding arrogance and verve of the immediate pre-Army recordings. These four CDs enclose the entire 'official' legacy of Elvis in the Fifties, but can't contain it: this music is so alive with the spirit of the unholy ghost that it constantly suggests new theories and permutations.

The fifth CD, subtitled 'Rare And Rockin',

proves once more that the RCA vaults are bottomless. Some of its contents are familiar to collectors – the Las Vegas hotel concert from 1956, for instance, two of the *Louisiana Hayride* recordings, and a couple of out-takes from the

'Essential' series, though this time taken from source tapes rather than battered acetates.

The rest, though, is brand new – and in some cases a revelation. For years, aficionados had believed that Elvis had recorded The Clovers' R&B hit, 'Fool, Fool, Fool', at Sun; and RCA had denied it. It turns out both sides were right: the tape existed, but it was cut in a studio in Lubbock, Texas, early in 1955, as a demo for possible use in Memphis. While Scotty Moore meanders aimlessly behind him, Elvis tests the limits of the material, as if considering this mid-pace blues song as a possible vehicle for 'Milkcow Blues Boogie' style mayhem. From the same source comes 'Shake, Rattle And Roll', not much removed from the arrangement Elvis used at RCA a year later, but carrying the same ghostly air of hillbilly music that cloaks all the Sun recordings.

Another insight into the Sun saga came with the first take of 'Blue Moon', which proves that Elvis came to the session with that unsettling, angelic arrangement already drifting through his mind. And there's one more slice of history, with the inclusion of what is claimed to be the last remaining off-cut from the 'Million Dollar Quartet' session – Elvis scatting his way through 'Reconsider Baby', while Jerry Lee Lewis tries to lead the band into 'Jingle Bells'.

The remaining RCA out-takes maybe aren't in that league – they don't match the best of the 'Essential' gems, in fact – but they have their moments, like the rinky-tink piano solo on an early take of 'Shake, Rattle And Roll', as if Russ Conway had crept in to the wrong session; and the sheer vitality of the alternate 'Lawdy Miss Clawdy'. How much more of this stuff is there in the vaults? Probably hours, or even dozens of hours: the next obvious step is entire albums of the sessions for particular songs. Until then, 'The Complete Fifties Masters' – beautifully packaged and annotated – is the last word on the pinnacle of Elvis's career.

1960-1968

Elvis reported for Army duty in Memphis on March 24, 1958. He was discharged on March 5, 1960, having been stationed in Arkansas, Texas and then West Germany. At Colonel Parker's insistence, he received little special treatment in the service, beyond the need to satisfy the interest of the world media in the Army's most famous recruit. He did what his country required, and convinced those who'd been scandalised by his on-stage *persona* that he was a simple, patriotic man who was – to quote the title of a cash-in single issued by country singer Bobby Bare in his absence – 'An All-American Boy'. He won credit for his willingness to toe the line, and sympathy when he was called home for his mother's funeral a few weeks before he was shipped to Germany.

His devotion to his country allowed Colonel Tom Parker to think of widening his charge's appeal. By maintaining a steady flow of positive news stories during Elvis's absence, and restricting RCA's release of new material to a trickle, Parker successfully built up an enormous demand for anything his boy did on his return.

Presley's fans were ready to welcome him with open arms; non-believers had never been more prepared to accept him as well. Parker took the loyalty of the teenage audience for granted, and set about trying to convert their elders. To that end, there were some changes on the horizon. The live performances which had thrust Elvis's hip-wiggling, pelvis-grinding antics to the fore were abandoned. Apart from two charity performances in 1961, Presley didn't appear on stage between 1958 and 1969. Parker was keen to attract an audience far larger than Elvis could ever satisfy on the concert circuit, by switching the focus of his activities to the movies.

There, too, there was a decisive shift of emphasis. Gone were the dramas of teenage angst and mild rebellion; in their place, Elvis was to become a wholesome film star for all the family, playing light comedy roles which required him to be good-humoured, fit and never more than a few minutes away from another song.

Musically, too, the direction switched, away from blues and country towards a more anodyne pop style. Elvis was no longer to be presented as a child of the South, steeped in the hillbilly heritage of Mississippi and Tennessee. Instead, he grew to artistic 'maturity' as an entertainer for the world, never affronting popular taste by making music that sounded uncomfortably intense or raw.

Tom Parker's deliberate obliteration of Elvis's 'natural' instincts towards rock'n'roll has won him a Machiavellian reputation – the musical equivalent of a man who strangles kittens for a living. But there's a case for his defence. First of all, Parker had no rock'n'roll blueprint to follow, no hint of what a teenage rebel could do apart from grow up or blow up. James Dean had done the latter; Marlon Brando the former. Elvis lacked Brando's willpower and assertiveness, and seems to have regarded Parker as a father-figure who could not be disobeyed. By setting up the template for future generations, Presley and Parker were breaking new ground – making rock history rather than continuing it. Elvis's example gave subsequent rock stars a role-model to follow or ignore. He had to live out the betrayal of the rock'n'roll dream, so that other generations could recognise it as a betrayal. And he himself – the man who loved Dean Martin's music as much as he did the blues – was a willing accomplice in the deal.

As we now know, Parker's choice of career for Elvis brought him unimagined international success; boredom; artistic decay; and the near-death of his commercial standing, reputation, and will to live. Instead of the electrifying rock'n'roll of the Fifties, Elvis spent almost all of the Sixties locked onto a treadmill of banal movies and equally lifeless music. But throughout it all, he remained the consummate entertainer – giving his best to even the most dispensable of his film songs.

THE POST-ARMY FILMS

After the hiatus of his Army service, Elvis resumed his movie career within two months – little realising when he arrived on the set of *G.I. Blues* in the first week of May 1960 that he was about to be plunged into a work-schedule as demanding and soul-destroying as anything he'd endured in uniform. In exactly nine years to the day, Elvis Presley made 27 Hollywood movies, grossing millions of dollars for all concerned, making him one of the most popular movie stars of the decade, and effectively sabotaging his previous career as a recording artist and live performer.

The best that can be said of Elvis's Sixties movies is that he survived them. Individually, they pass the time smoothly enough; the plots are no more lame or obvious than any other teen exploitation films of the era. Taken in bulk, however, they cast an eerie shadow across his life. In his prime as a vocalist and performer, he was condemned to waste little less than a decade on ventures that were nothing more than artistic candy floss. It's as if Charles Dickens had abandoned his writing for ten years to concoct advertising slogans for his local butcher.

Ironies abound when you examine the movie years more closely. Without having to leave the twin bases of Memphis and Hollywood, Elvis entertained more people with his films than he could ever have done in person, regardless of how gruelling was his touring schedule. For at least four years, the movies provided him with a constant succession of hit singles and gold albums; a public profile unmatched by any other pop artists until The Beatles; and an income far beyond any of his rivals. The movies ended not because Presley rebelled against them, but because the ticket sales didn't any longer justify the film companies' investment. If Elvis had made better movies, especially after 1965, then his film career might actually have been prolonged, and the artistic renaissance of his musical efforts after 1968 might never have happened. Most bizarre of all, the enervating, production-line stream of films which nearly killed his career had the opposite effect on his personal life. Only when the comforting framework of regular Hollywood shoots was removed did Elvis briefly flourish, in the studio and on the road, and then lapse into years of mixed boredom and depression, which culminated in his death at the age of 42. Success and artistic fulfilment are never quite as straightforward as they seem in Elvis Presley's career.

Music was central to almost every movie Elvis made in the Sixties. Sadly, with the pick of the world's songwriters at his disposal, Colonel Parker elected to commission Elvis's film songs from a small coterie of insiders, few of whom showed any awareness of the rapid changes taking place in the pop world beyond Hollywood. This, finally, is what made the Presey movies so appalling. The world could have stood tired scripts and lacklustre acting, but a continuous parade of hackneyed, gormless and lifeless musical numbers quickly turned Elvis's movie career into a farce. As the numerous outtakes from the soundtrack sessions prove, Elvis Presley was as aware of this debacle as anyone. He simply lacked the power, or the will, to do anything about it.

G.I. BLUES (1960)

A cynical cash-in on Elvis's well-publicised stint in the US Army, *G.I. Blues* was filmed on the Paramount Studios lot, but set in West Germany, in a fictionalised version of Elvis's own barracks. The mild shenanigans of the plot allowed Elvis – alias Tulsa McLean, the cheeky G.I. with the heart of (what else?) gold – to perform 11 songs, suitably collated on the soundtrack album. For the first time, Elvis's film music was subjugated to the demands of the plot, with songs like 'Big Boots' and 'Frankfort Special' having no independent life outside the movie.

The clearest indication of what the movies would do to Elvis's music came with the re-make of his 1956 classic 'Blue Suede Shoes', here reduced to a tame, toothless pop-rocker that wouldn't have been out of place on a Frankie Avalon album. It certainly had nothing to do with rock'n'roll, and neither did the movie. The sentimental 'Wooden Heart' – sung to a puppet, no less – proved to be a popular choice of single in Britain, and provides a far more accurate clue to what's contained on the LP.

One of the better CD transfers from Elvis's first decade at RCA. Alternate versions of three tracks can be heard on 'Collectors Gold'.

FLAMING STAR (1960)

Flaming Star was Presley's first film away from Paramount, under the auspices of Twentieth-Century Fox. And give them credit, Fox (with the aid of director Don Siegel) did set out to make a movie, rather than an Elvis movie. Initial plans to co-star Marlon Brando alongside Presley

fell through, but the surprisingly tough action in this Western left little room for music. Just two numbers, the title song and 'A Cane And A High Starched Collar', were included in the film; two more, 'Britches' and 'Summer Kisses, Winter Tears', were cut from the final print. In fact, 'Britches' and 'A Cane...' weren't released on record until the mid-Seventies.

Not yet available on CD in coherent form. The provisional title tune for the movie, 'Black Star', surfaced for the first time on 'Collectors Gold', alongside an alternate 'Summer Kisses, Winter Tears'.

WILD IN THE COUNTRY (1961)

For the last time in eight years, *Wild In The Country* provided Elvis with a movie vehicle that was more than a jog-trotting exploitation of his international success. Torn by his varying degrees of involvement with three women, Elvis's character has to admit to adult emotions – not apparent in any of his movies after this point until *Charro* in 1969. Just four songs were included in the film, and one of those ('Husky Dusky Day') never made the recording studio. Of the rest, the title track became a single B-side, the amiable 'I Slipped, I Stumbled, I Fell' surfaced quickly on the 'Something For Everybody' LP, and the delicate ballad 'In My Way' was eventually salvaged on 'Elvis For Everyone' in 1965.

Available on CD only haphazardly. Different versions of 'I Slipped . . .' and 'Lonely Man' were unveiled on 'Collectors Gold'.

BLUE HAWAII (1961)

Returning to Paramount, Elvis went out on location for the first of his 'tourism' movies – pictures that cast their star as just one more beautiful and exotic sight in a pageant of unusual sounds and visions. At its peak, *Blue Hawaii* was the second highest-grossing film in America, and its success signed the death warrant on Elvis's acting aspirations. Its lightly romantic, mildly appealing formula was followed like a blueprint in his subsequent films.

The soundtrack album boasted some 14 songs, of which two (the twist number 'Rock-A-Hula Baby' and the wonderful ballad, 'Can't Help Falling In Love') were paired on a hit single. The rest is pure confection, from start to finish – mostly tinged with the trappings of the Hawaiian location, and little of it bearable beyond the confines of the movie.

Available as a single CD, this is very listenable in terms of sound quality, if not always on musical grounds.

FOLLOW THAT DREAM (1962)

The location moved from Hawaii to Florida, and the songs were chopped from 14 to five, but otherwise *Follow That Dream* was another pleasant, unmemorable step in Elvis's decline. As a sign of the way things were heading, the film started life as *Pioneer, Go Home*, until Colonel Parker's team of willing composers announced they were stuck for convincing rhymes for 'pioneer'.

In the event, 'Follow That Dream' proved to be one of the more memorable Elvis title themes – lightweight, perhaps, but

sung with the smooth assurance of a master vocalist. (In vastly reworked form, it subsequently became something of a live anthem for Presley fan Bruce Springsteen in the early Eighties.) The song headed up the pleasant soundtrack EP, which thankfully didn't feature one song briefly aired in the film: 'On Top Of Ole Smokey'.

Not yet issued on CD in one package. Check 'Collectors Gold' for alternate takes of 'What A Wonderful Life' and the throwaway 'A Whistling Tune'.

KID GALAHAD (1962)

Originally a vehicle for Edward G. Robinson, Bette Davis and Humphrey Bogart in 1937, *Kid Galahad* was not an ideal subject for a musical, centring as it did around the somewhat tawdry adventures of a boxer. The consensus amongst the Presley entourage was that such an aggressive role, even in a smoothed-out revamp of the original plot, worked against the hard-built Elvis image. Instead, Elvis passed the tough-guy mantle to one of his supporting players, Charles Bronson.

For the first time, there was no title song for this movie: instead, the credits rolled to the sound of the fairly convincing rocker 'King Of The Whole Wide World'. It was by far the strongest song on the soundtrack EP, though another tune from this film, 'I Got Lucky', was later used to head up a budget Presley LP.

All six songs – three of them in longer-than-usual versions – are available on a 'Double Features' CD, coupled with the 'Girls! Girls! Girls' soundtrack.

GIRLS! GIRLS! GIRLS! (1962)

No beating about the bush this time: the title announced that Elvis was playing the lead in a romantic comedy, and his irresistible charms were attracting an entourage. True, the plot went a little further than that – Elvis was a singer running a charter fishing service – but not much further. As far as the back-room bandits were concerned, the movie was all about songs, and there were plenty of them on offer.

No fewer than 13 surfaced during the 106 minutes of the movie, and all but one (a reprise of the title track) made the soundtrack album. These included the massive hit single 'Return To Sender', the ultra-cool, ultra-tender ballad 'Where Do You Come From', and plenty of plot-forwarding junk like 'Thanks To The Rolling Sea' and 'Song Of The Shrimp'. Amazingly, the title song was an R&B comedy number originally cut by The Coasters; even more amazingly, no fewer than four extra songs were cut from the movie in the final stages.

Extra songs like 'Mama', 'Plantation Rock', 'Dainty Little Moonbeams' and the end titles version of the title track are all included alongside the standard film numbers on a 'Double Features' CD – coupled with the soundtrack music from 'Kid Galahad'.

IT HAPPENED AT THE WORLD'S FAIR (1963)

The World's Fair in question took place in Seattle in 1962, and Elvis actually travelled to the West Coast to take advantage of the temporary locations. One scene even took place in the city's prime landmark, the restaurant of the Space Needle. But the most exciting episode of the movie came when Elvis was kicked by a small boy played by one Kurt Russell – who 16 years later ended up playing the part of the King in *Elvis – The Movie*.

MGM Films (this was their first Elvis movie) and Colonel Parker scraped together 10 songs for this flimsy comic drama. Without a single gem to their credit, they assembled these as a low-value, low-interest soundtrack LP, which ran for little more than 20 minutes. The tie-in single, 'One Broken Heart For Sale', duly became one of the shortest records ever to make the Top 20. Its flip-side, the gentle 'They Remind Me Too Much Of You', was the artistic zenith of a dreadful album.

The entire soundtrack LP – plus the film version of 'One Broken Heart For Sale' – is included on a 'Double Features' CD with the songs from 'Fun In Acapulco'. An alternate 'Beyond The Bend' and a longer 'One Broken Heart For Sale' appear on 'Collectors Gold'.

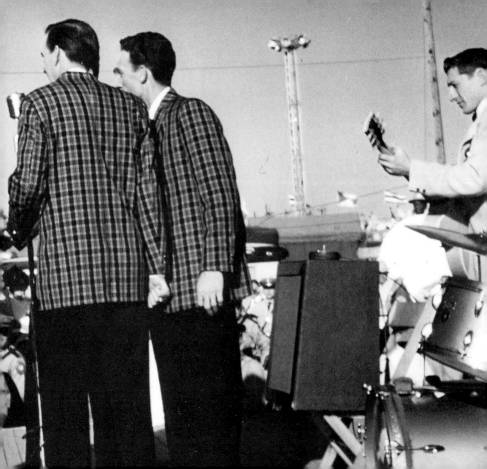

FUN IN ACAPULCO (1963)

Even the first US film appearance of Swiss actress Ursula Andress didn't make Elvis's Mexican musical memorable. All of his scenes were shot in Hollywood, so the film was understandably light on atmosphere – and on drama, unless the romantic adventures of a trapeze artist turned lifeguard raise your blood pressure.

True to form, there was a soundtrack LP, which included a wonderful period piece of a hit single, the dance novelty 'Bossa Nova Baby'. Also on board, though, were some of the loudest turkeys of Elvis's movie career, like 'There's No Room To Rhumba In A Sports Car' and 'The Bullfighter Was A Lady'. Perhaps realising that they couldn't rip off the public twice in a row, RCA added two 'bonus songs' to the LP, 'Love Me Tonight' and 'Slowly but Surely', both taped back in Nashville.

All the film songs, but not the two bonus cuts, are on a 'Double Features' CD, alongside the soundtrack of 'It Happened At The World's Fair'.

KISSIN' COUSINS (1964)

More amusing than most of Elvis's Sixties musicals, *Kissin' Cousins* had its star playing twin roles as lookalike relations Josh Morgan and Jodie Tatum. Singer and Presley buddy Lance Le Gault doubled for Elvis in the shots where both characters appeared simultaneously.

Besides the nine songs in the picture (including two different arrangements of the rockin' title track), the soundtrack LP included some bonus songs — 'Anyone' (taped for the film but chopped from the final cut), 'Echoes Of Love' and 'Long Lonely Highway'. The last of these songs, probably the best of a weak bunch, surfaced again as a single B-side more than a year later.

Not available on CD outside Japan.

VIVA LAS VEGAS (1964)

This movie was retitled *Love In Las Vegas* for British consumption – the UK distributors presumably reckoning that local audiences would be baffled by a title that didn't have a single word in decent, respectable English. The frantic dance rhythms of the original title track still made it into the British Top 20, however, Spanish words or not.

Strangely, RCA elected not to issue a soundtrack album from this movie, despite its stronger than usual musical content. Besides the almost rocking title track, there was an energetic cover of Ray Charles' 'What'd I Say', a bouncy number called 'C'mon Everybody' (not the Eddie Cochran song, sadly), and a smoochy ballad in 'I Need Somebody To Lean On'. After that, the inclusion of a weary medley of 'The Yellow Rose Of Texas' and 'The Eyes Of Texas' could almost be forgiven.

Things could have been better still: the movie was originally meant to feature a lively duet with co-star Ann-Margret, 'The Lady Loves Me', plus the dance tune 'Do The Vega'. Like 'Night Life', they were chopped from the film – and the meagre soundtrack EP. So too was 'You're The Boss', another duet, and one of the raunchiest movie cuts of the Sixties.

All 10 songs connected with this film are available on a 'Double Features' CD with the 'Roustabout' soundtrack. 'You're The Boss' is also on 'Collectors Gold'.

ROUSTABOUT (1964)

Find a location, recycle an old script, let the songs carry the plot, wind up the key in Elvis's back and presto! – another Presley movie. *Roustabout* switched the locale to a carnival, enabling the hack composers to churn out numbers like 'Carny Town' and 'It's Carnival Time'. There was a brief nod to Elvis's past via a recreation of The Coasters' R&B novelty, 'Little Egypt', but otherwise the distressingly short soundtrack LP was filled with songs that were purely functional, and had no independent life outside the context of the film. There wasn't even a hit single in the package. The album still topped the American charts, but proved to be Elvis's last No. 1 LP of the Sixties.

All 11 songs meet the 10 from 'Viva Las Vegas' on a 'Double Features' CD. A different version of the title track surfaced on 'Collectors Gold'.

GIRL HAPPY (1965)

'See How Youth Reacts When The Gates Are Opened', screamed MGM's advertising slogan for Elvis's 17th movie. So was *Girl Happy* a searing insight into contemporary teenage sexual habits? Not exactly. Elvis was chosen as a chaperone for some young women (clever choice) and met up with some gangsters. Cue such memorable songs as 'Fort Lauderdale Chamber Of Commerce' and the elegantly titled 'Do The Clam', one of the decade's less successful dance crazes.

To fill out the soundtrack LP, RCA added an out-take from 1962, 'You'll Be Gone'. Both 'Do The Clam' and 'Puppet On A String' (not the Sandie Shaw hit) were extracted as singles, but do you remember them? I thought not.

The 11 soundtrack songs can be found alongside those from 'Harum Scarum' on one of the 'Double Features' CDs. An alternate take of the title track was included on 'Collectors Gold'.

TICKLE ME (1965)

Rodeos, buried treasure, ghosts – all in the same forgettable movie. *Tickle Me* was Elvis's first film for Allied Artists, and also his last. It was memorable for quite another reason, though: for the only time, no new songs were prepared for the soundtrack. Instead, nine previously released recordings were introduced into the plot, among them such highlights of 1960's 'Elvis Is Back' LP as 'Dirty, Dirty Feeling' and 'It Feels So Right'. RCA included five of the songs on a soundtrack EP, then bowed to public demand in Britain and slapped the four leftovers onto a second extended-play single. But all the tracks are now available on other CDs.

HARUM SCARUM (1965)

Harum Scarum – or *Harem Holiday*, as it was bizarrely retitled in Britain – was centred around the same basic idea as The Beatles' *Help!*, being filmed at exactly the same time. In both movies, a pop star is being threatened by assassins of a Middle Eastern persuasion. Both films are musicals; both filled thousands of cinemas around the world.

But there the comparisons end: *Help!* had some brilliant songs, *Harum Scarum* had none, as titles like 'My Desert Serenade', 'Go East, Young Man' and 'Kismet' suggest. The soundtrack LP featured 11 forgettable movie numbers, without a hit single in sight.

The entire soundtrack is featured on a 'Double Features' CD, with the songs from 'Girl Happy'. An alternate 'So Close, Yet So Far' appears on 'Collectors Gold'.

FRANKIE AND JOHNNY (1966)

Loosely based on the 19th century folksong, and a 1930s movie of the same title, *Frankie And Johnny* had Elvis playing a riverboat gambler on the *SS Mississippi Queen* (conveniently docked in the MGM Studios). In keeping with the vaguely pre-war feel, Elvis concocted a trad jazz medley of 'Down By The Riverside' and 'The Saints Go Marching In', plus a souped-up revamp of the title song.

The remaining soundtrack songs ranged from the mildly attractive ('Please Don't Stop Loving Me') to the frankly disposable

('Petunia The Gardener's Daughter'). 'Chesay' was a duet with some passing gypsies, while numbers like 'Come Along', 'Shout It Out' and 'Everybody Come Aboard' were tired movie fodder, there purely to highlight the lukewarm action. *Not yet available on CD.*

PARADISE, HAWAIIAN STYLE (1966)

Or how to remake *Blue Hawaii* without trying – at all. Elvis is a pilot who starts a helicopter service and meets some Hawaiian girls: end of story. Along the way, he mimes to some of the most mindless songs on any Presley album, among them the laughable 'A Dog's Life', 'Queenie Wahini's Papaya' and the unforgettable 'Scratch My Back (Then I'll Scratch Yours)'. The soundtrack album returned to the bad old days of 'It Happened At The World's Fair', barely scraping past the 20-minute mark. Elvis movies and their music don't come much worse than this.

Thankfully, perhaps, yet to be issued on CD.

SPINOUT (1966)

In their constant quest to portray Elvis as a man of action and romance, his film producers regularly cast him as a racing driver. *Spinout* – retitled *California Holiday* by British distributors who presumably felt the UK audience couldn't cope with even the most basic American slang – was at least more lively than *Paradise, Hawaiian Style*, with a soundtrack to match. This time, the composers at least sounded as if they'd been listening to other recent US teen musicals, giving songs like 'Stop, Look And Listen' and 'Adam And Evil' a vaguely contemporary feel.

That doesn't excuse the dreadful 'Smorgasbord', of course, but anyone who bought the soundtrack album was in for a surprise treat. Tacked on to the end of the nine film songs were three bonus cuts, the ballad 'I'll Remember You' and two gems – the best performances on any Elvis movie LP since 'King Creole'. 'Down In The Alley' was a gritty piece of R&B, that sounded as if Elvis had been listening to what Stax Records had been recording just down the road from Graceland; while

'Tomorrow Is A Long Time' was, miracle of miracles, a Bob Dylan song, which the songwriter chose as his favourite interpretation of his own material in a subsequent interview.

Another soundtrack awaiting CD transfer in full, though alternate takes of 'Stop, Look And Listen' and 'Am I Ready' can be sampled on 'Collectors Gold'.

EASY COME, EASY GO (1967)

From the nearly sublime to the utterly ridiculous, *Easy Come, Easy Go* reviewed itself in its title. Elvis played a frogman, and must have wished he could stay underwater when he heard the songs delivered by Colonel Parker's team of diehards. If there's a more muddle-headed and pathetic song on the planet than 'Yoga Is As Yoga Does', then thankfully I've never heard it. 'The Love Machine' and 'You Gotta Stop' were a notch or two up the evolutionary ladder, but still embarrassing, especially when it became apparent that they were supposed to sound hip.

Coming four months after Elvis's most productive studio session in years, these

tracks were a disastrous step backwards. RCA issued an EP of the film songs, but no-one who heard them first bought it.
Last in the queue for CD release.

had already been issued as B-sides over the previous couple of years.
Unissued on CD in full.

DOUBLE TROUBLE (1967)

Partly set in London and Belgium, *Double Trouble* was entirely filmed in California. So much for authenticity, then, and also for creativity. "Elvis takes mad mod Europe by storm", so MGM's film poster claimed, "as he swings into a brand new adventure filled with dames, diamonds, discotheques and danger." It was also filled with lousy songs, including the beer-festival singalong, 'I Love Only One Girl', and one of the nadirs of Presley's career – 'Old MacDonald', sung to a truck-load of chickens.

In retrospect, the most ironic moment in this movie comes at the start, when Guy 'Elvis' Lambert performs at "a London nightclub" – the closest he ever came to playing a concert in Britain.

With only eight songs in the film, RCA filled up the soundtrack LP with oldies, two of which ('Blue River' and 'Never Ending')

CLAMBAKE (1967)

Elvis wasn't the only star in *Clambake*: Flipper the dolphin (main player in a popular US TV series) also made an appearance. Flipper didn't sing – probably a wise move, judging by the quality of the material Elvis was given for the soundtrack. There was one glorious exception, in the shape of 'You Don't Know Me', an early Sixties crossover hit by R&B/country star Ray Charles. Elvis delivered a precise, reasonably involved version of the song, which far outstripped trivia like the children's singalong, 'Confidence', and the banal 'Hey, Hey, Hey'.

The 'Clambake' LP was saved by its bonus material, which included the R&B-styled single, 'Big Boss Man', the country song 'Just Call Me Lonesome', and the film reject 'How Can You Lose What You Never Had'. 'Big Boss Man' was the real prize, but was handily issued as a single, backed by the only other

essential cut, 'You Don't Know Me'.

The bonus songs are on 'From Nashville To Memphis', but not the movie tracks. Anyone desperate to hear an alternate version of 'How Can You Lose What You Never Had' should try 'Collectors Gold'.

STAY AWAY, JOE (1968)

Shock, horror – there was no soundtrack album this time; in fact, not even a soundtrack single. *Stay Away, Joe* had just five songs, and one of them ('Lovely Mamie' had just one vocal line). Another, an ode to a bull called Dominick, was never issued by RCA. That left three above-average efforts: 'Stay Away', 'Stay Away, Joe' (on one memorable occasion, RCA confused the two songs and issued the wrong one on a budget LP) and the fine 'All I Needed Was The Rain'. True, the movie was still dreadful, but the Arizona locations were a change from the inside of the MGM lot. *Not yet available on CD.*

SPEEDWAY (1968)

For the first time, Elvis appeared alongside another singing star in *Speedway* – Nancy Sinatra, who'd enjoyed two No. 1 hits since 1966 (two more than Elvis, incidentally). As reward, she was allowed her own solo performance in the movie and on the soundtrack LP, besides duetting with Elvis on 'There Ain't Nothin' Like A Song'. As a low-luck, high-charm racing driver,

Elvis got to pose in a Dodge Charger throughout the movie, besides starring in the by now obligatory discotheque scene, where he romped through the ersatz rocker, 'Let Yourself Go'.

Nothing else on the soundtrack had much to commend it, so RCA made up the weight with a bunch of bonus tunes. 'Five Sleepy Heads' had been cut from the film, but the rest were comparatively recent studio efforts – except for 'Western Union', which had been resting in the vaults since 1963.

Still awaiting full release on CD.

LIVE A LITTLE, LOVE A LITTLE (1968)

Such was the parlous state of Elvis Presley's career by late 1968 that this movie – starring Elvis as a photographer with an eye for the girls, amazingly enough – wasn't issued in Britain. With just four songs in the movie, there was no call for a soundtrack release. Instead, 'Wonderful World' was slipped onto a budget LP called 'Flaming Star' at the end of 1968, while another *Live A Little* number,

'Almost In Love', became the title track of another budget LP, where it was joined by the remaining film songs, 'Edge Of Reality' and 'A Little Less Conversation'. All four songs showed welcome signs of maturity, if not yet overt class.

Not available on CD in one package.

CHARRO (1969)

For his first Western since *Flaming Star*, Elvis was given a script that required him not only to grow a beard, but also to play a serious role, as an ex-outlaw seeking revenge after being framed for one crime he actually didn't commit. Elvis sang the title song, a moody ballad which was hidden away on the flipside of a single, and then remained musically silent for the duration of the picture. Instead, the film music was supplied by Hugo Montenegro, who at the time he began scoring the movie was enjoying a No. 1 hit with his theme to *The Good, The Bad And The Ugly*.

'Charro' remains unissued on UK or European CD.

THE TROUBLE WITH GIRLS (1969)

Long before *Charro* reached the screen, Elvis had begun work on *The Trouble With Girls*, set in 1927, in which Presley played the manager of a travelling medicine show who unwittingly falls into a murderous situation. Part comedy, part drama, the movie was a return to the musical format – though without the tie-in record releases. 'Clean Up Your Own Backyard' was pulled from the film as a minor hit single, but of the rest, only 'Almost' was released during Elvis's lifetime.

Not issued as a package on CD.

CHANGE OF HABIT (1969)

Elvis's final dramatic role came in this socially aware drama, in which he played a doctor whose horizons are widened by a group of nuns, among them comedy star Mary Tyler Moore. If the film was bizarre, its musical content was far more orthodox, marking the fact that Elvis's movie songs had finally caught up with his studio work. One of the film songs, 'Rubberneckin' ', was taped during his legendary sessions at American Studios in Memphis, while the rest of the soundtrack followed just two weeks after the last of those American sessions, and retained much of their vocal power. Only 'Rubberneckin' ' reached the shops during the year the film was released, however.

Not released as a set of songs on CD.

THE SINGLES 1960-1968

Elvis's first single after leaving the Army – his first for almost a year – was 'Stuck On You', which immediately raced to the top of the charts. It could almost have been designed by committee, as its jog-trot rhythm hinted at the rock'n'roll of the past, without any unpleasant raucousness. Rock'n'roll fans remember the slight tinge of disappointment, which they excused by assuming that Elvis was feeling his way back towards his music. Instead, 'Stuck On You' was followed by 'It's Now Or Never', a gloriously mock-operatic treatment of an Italian ballad; and 'Are You Lonesome Tonight', a sentimental love song with a banal narration. The shift away from 'A Big Hunk O'Love' and 'One Night' was sudden and dramatic.

Within five years, the brilliantly sung pop songs of 1960 and 1961 began to take on the misty glow of a golden era, as Elvis was submerged in a morass of fatuous movie songs and ill-considered dance tunes. The soundtrack sessions began as a sideline to Presley's studio work, but by 1965 they had buried it. With three movies a year to be completed, there was little time for 'serious' recording. Elvis managed one non-movie session apiece in 1962 and 1963; one, which spawned just three songs, in 1964; and none at all in 1965. Only in 1966, when Elvis's singles were struggling to reach the Top 20, did he stage a major studio session again.

Such traumas seemed an unlikely prospect in the early Sixties, when everything Elvis sang turned to gold. In 1960 and 1961, there was still an edge to his voice – an affirmation of life – that gave his pop songs a sense of danger. His first single of 1961 was the Italian song 'Surrender', another venture into the waters of light opera which required remarkable vocal control and range, and which Elvis sang as if he'd been born for that purpose alone.

Over the next two years, he issued a succession of innocuous but charming pop songs, some taken from movies, some not, but united by the elegance of Elvis's performance. Mingled among 'His Latest Flame', 'She's Not You' and 'Return To Sender' was the occasional rocker like 'I Feel So Bad', and a ballad like 'Can't Help Falling In Love', which carried far more emotional weight than his similar work in the Fifties.

By 1963, however, film songs were beginning to dominate the release schedule. 'One Broken Heart For Sale', 'Bossa Nova Baby' and 'Kissin' Cousins' still had that voice, but no hint of inspiration in the songwriting. The frenetic 'Viva Las Vegas' was a step in the right direction, but it didn't reach the Top 20. Elvis was suffering by comparison with the abrupt shift in the American pop world after January 1964, when The Beatles inaugurated 'The British Invasion'. Inspired by the way Elvis *used* to sound, The Beatles and their beat group cohorts rekindled the raucousness and amateur enthusiasm of Fifties rock'n'roll, leaving Elvis sounding middle-aged by comparison.

Some of his biggest hits in the mid-Sixties came with old recordings – RCA reviving 'Such A Night' and 'Crying In The Chapel' from 1960, and the previously unreleased 'Ain't That Lovin' You Baby' from as far back as 1958. Then, the song had been considered too poor to release; by 1964, it was starting to sound like vintage Elvis.

In 1965, things got worse; another Fifties leftover, 'Tell Me Why', had to be dragged out as a single. It took the Nashville studio sessions of May 1966 to nudge Elvis away from the movie treadmill into some kind of awareness of where his talents were best directed. Only one single came from those sessions, a delicate reading of 'Love Letters', but it was Elvis's best 45 in years.

After another 12 months of movie singles, there came a breakthrough. In September 1967, guitarist and songwriter Jerry Reed was invited to join Elvis at RCA Studios in Nashville. He guided Presley through a beefy version of a R&B stan-dard, 'Big Boss Man', and also offered a made-to-order country rock tune, 'Guitar Man'. With Reed's driving guitar to the fore, Elvis turned in one of his most involved performances of the decade. By this point, his reputation had slipped to the point that not even this fabulous record could breach the Top 40. But a follow-up in the same style, Reed's 'US Male', did make No. 28. After five years of movie madness, Elvis Presley was learning how to function as a recording artist once again. What's more, he sounded contemporary – if not amidst the psychedelic chaos of California, then in the country charts of Nashville.

ELVIS' GOLDEN RECORDS VOL. 3 (1963)

Everything on this 12-track album had appeared on one side or other of a Top 5 single, easily justifying the title. Within the limitations of the short running time, it's hard to imagine a more representative selection of Elvis's career immediately after he left the Army.

Far superior sound on this CD to its two

predecessors in the 'Golden Records' series.

ELVIS' GOLDEN RECORDS VOL. 4 (1968)

Few of Presley's singles since 1963 had actually achieved gold status, so RCA had to cheat a little this time around. They scraped together a collection of early Sixties B-sides (including the sublime 1960 cut, 'A Mess Of Blues' and 1963's fine ballad, 'It Hurts Me'), and some of the more successful mid-Sixties 45s, like 'Love Letters'. But the compilers probably cheated a little to class 1967's 'Indescribably Blue as a 'gold record', when it had failed to reach the Top 30.

Variable track listing, but again impressively consistent sound.

THE ALBUMS 1960-1968

Between Elvis's re-emergence from the Army in March 1960, and the airing of his NBC TV Special in December 1968, RCA issued 23 Presley albums in America. No fewer than 15 of those were film soundtracks; a further two were compilations; leaving just six LPs of original studio material in more than eight years. No wonder that fans complained that Elvis regarded his music as an afterthought in the Sixties.

For confirmation, check the titles of three of those records: 'Something For Everybody', 'Pot Luck' and 'Elvis For Everyone'. On the one hand, they pledged allegiance to the widest possible musical canvas; on the other, they betrayed the haphazard method of their compilation. It took the three remaining LPs to convey some kind of certainty – either via the religious faith of 'His Hand In Mine' and 'How Great Thou Art', or the confident assertion that 'Elvis Is Back'. And so he was, but not for long.

ELVIS IS BACK (1960)

In many ways, 'Elvis Is Back' was the perfect Presley album. That didn't make it his best, his hardest-rocking, his most mature or his most successful. But it encapsulated within 12 songs everything that Elvis had been, and meant, during the Fifties, and everything that he would become across the following decade. After 'Elvis Is Back', everyone should have known what was going to happen next, and the extent of what they were about to lose.

The album was recorded in just four days of studio work, spread across two weeks. These were the first post-Army sessions, and (ironically enough) his last recordings for almost eight years to capture the excitement and thrill of his best Fifties sides. Surrounded by friends like Scotty Moore, D.J. Fontana, The Jordanaires and Hank Garland, augmented by top saxman Boots Randolph, Floyd Cramer and Buddy Harman, Elvis let rip. He never cut grittier blues tunes at any stage of his career than 'Reconsider Baby' or 'It Feels So Right'; never exposed his teasing, inviting sexuality as blatantly as he did on 'Fever' or the sizzling cover of the Johnnie Ray hit, 'Such A Night'; and never sang pure pop songs with the playful glee which he invested in 'The Girl Of My Best Friend' and 'Dirty, Dirty Feeling'. And on 'Soldier Boy' and 'I Will Be Home Again', he made plain that he could out-

sentimentalise anyone in showbusiness without ever sounding an iota less than utterly sincere.

It was a brilliant record, which suggested that nothing was beyond his grasp. It conjured up the vision of a performer who could be all things to all men (and women) – a flirtatious teenage idol with a heart of gold, a tempestuous, dangerous lover; a gutbucket blues singer; a sophisticated nightclub entertainer; and the raucous rocker he'd already proved himself to be. This was growing older with style, adapting to the restrictions of adulthood and fame without shedding a fraction of his soul. If he'd continued in this vein, he could have had it all: No. 1 records, family appeal, and the threatening glint of a teen rebel in his eyes. He might even have pre-empted the need for the British Invasion. The secret message of 'Elvis Is Back' is "what might be" – which quickly soured into "what might have been".

Apart from a mastering fault at the beginning of 'Soldier Boy', reducing the length of the track by a second or two, this magnificent album sounds suitably impressive on CD. It appears in full on 'From Nashville To Memphis'.

HIS HAND IN MINE (1960)

Many commentators on Elvis's career have seen his gospel recordings as evidence of the betrayal of his rock'n'roll roots. In this theory, gospel equals religious, which equals conservative, which equals the opposite of rock'n'roll. By singing songs of faith instead of rebellion, these critics argue, he was undermining the power and the glory of his career as a rock'n'roll pioneer.

It's a convincing enough theory, until you remember Elvis's roots – or simply *listen* to the gospel recordings. Social life and the church are indissolubly linked in the American South, in a way that's difficult to comprehend in Britain. Raising Elvis in the church wasn't a decision for the Presleys, it was an automatic process. Equally automatic is the place of singing within the Southern church tradition. Black and white churches resound to lifted voices of praise from choirs, quartets and soloists. Across the South, there was a lengthy tradition of male vocal quartets, which spawned R&B singers like Sam Cooke, Jackie Wilson and Clyde McPhatter, and which came close to claiming the young Elvis Presley in 1954. That was the year he signed to Sun – and then, a few weeks later, was approached by the prestigious Blackwood Brothers quartet to join their second-string line-up, The Songfollows. Under contract to Sam Phillips at Sun, Elvis had to decline; if the Blackwoods had approached him six months earlier, he might have been lost to secular music forever.

As numerous biographies and documentary films have pointed out, Elvis regularly relaxed by singing gospel songs with anyone who was around. It's no coincidence that the bulk of the so-called Million Dollar Quartet recordings featuring Elvis, Carl Perkins and Jerry Lee Lewis have these three God-fearing Southern boys singing gospel rather than rhythm & blues.

Elvis made his first tentative step into gospel recording early in 1957, when he recorded the 'Peace In The Valley' EP at the same session as his 'All Shook Up' single. At the end of October 1960, he devoted two days of recording to an extended gospel project – producing the 'His Hand In Mine' album, plus the 'Surrender' single and (bizarrely) 'Crying In The Chapel', omitted from the 1960 LP and held back from release until 1965, when it duly became one of his biggest hit singles.

The repertoire on the album was evenly divided between spiritual songs that had been popular for decades, even centuries ('I'm Gonna Walk Dem Golden Stairs', 'Milky White Way', 'Swing Down, Sweet Chariot') and contemporary material composed in the Fifties ('In My Father's House', 'Known Only To Him', 'Working On The Building'). Exquisitely sung, with vocal support from The Jordanaires, the album ranged from delicate ballads to fervent celebrations of faith that in a different context could be said to hint at rock.

On the UK CD, 'His Hand In Mine' comes with three bonus tracks: 'It Is No Secret' (from the 'Peace In The Valley' EP of 1957); 'Who Am I' (from the Memphis sessions in 1969); and 'You'll Never Walk Alone' (taped in 1967).

SOMETHING FOR EVERYBODY (1961)

'Something For Everybody' was the boast, which translated on vinyl to something for lovers of ballads and soft-rock'n'roll. Cut almost entirely in two days of sessions in March 1961, Elvis's second post-Army album was a prime early example of what came to be known as 'the Nashville Sound'. This tasteful, restrained approach, epitomised by the sporadic flourishes of Floyd Cramer's piano, came to dominate the world of country music in the Sixties, effectively masking the genre's rural origins. It provided much the same service for Elvis, producing an album that had hints of rock but little sign that the singer had been raised on blues and hillbilly.

On vinyl, the LP was divided between a side of ballads and another of what passed for rock'n'roll. Had it been recorded for 'Elvis Is Back', 'Give Me The Right' would have reeked of rhythm and blues, but on this album both Elvis and the band held back, reducing a powerful vehicle to a slow crawl. And that was as tough as any of the ballads got, with the remainder living up to one of the song titles: 'Gently'. The singing, as ever, was perfect, but utterly removed from the Presley who'd recorded for Sun. Flip the original album over, and some of Elvis's rock raunch was intact. 'I'm Coming Home' belonged to the same melodic school as Nat 'King' Cole's hit, 'Mona Lisa', while the moody, echo-laden 'I Want You With Me' rasped with a little of the menace of 'Trouble' from the 'King Creole' soundtrack. The rest was a pleasant, unthreatening pastiche of the music that had once been Elvis's birthright.

The CD reproduces the original album in style.

POT LUCK (1962)

The menu diversified on Elvis's next album, but all the meat dishes were off. Rock'n'roll was expunged from Elvis's repertoire, in other words, and replaced by a strangely diverse mix of pop styles – several with a Latin flavour, from the baion beat that pulsed through 'Fountain Of

Love' to the Mexican aroma of the unbelievably square ballad, 'I'm Yours'. Purring exquisitely through 'Something Blue', or teasing flirtatiously on 'Kiss Me Quick', Elvis sounded as threatening as a neutered tomcat. 'Gonna Get Back Home Somehow' hinted at where he'd come from, but overall 'Pot Luck' was decidedly less raucous than the records Del Shannon, Gene Pitney and Roy Orbison were making at the same time. It still had its moments, though, from the glorious pop paranoia of 'Suspicion' (an obvious hit single in waiting, as Terry Stafford proved when he covered it in 1964) to the classy pop beat of 'Night Rider'. And then there was the stunningly beautiful 'That's Someone You'll Never Forget', commissioned by Elvis from his friend Red West as a tribute to his late mother. Eerie and unforgettable, this delicate ballad oozed emotion being held tightly under restraint — completely unlike the rest of the album, where emotion never came into the equation.

Fine CD sound quality helps make up for the lack of artistic passion.

ELVIS FOR EVERYONE (1965)

1965 was the year when Elvis recorded nothing but film songs. In the absence of a soundtrack album for the *Tickle Me* movie, however, RCA needed another Presley album – especially as sales of his singles were beginning to slide.

The result was this curious collection, which gathered together offcuts from ten years of studio sessions. Although there was nothing in the package to say so, 'Elvis For Everyone' actually included three pre-Army recordings, one of which actually dated back to his time with Sam Phillips at Sun. That was 'Tomorrow Night', a blues ballad which hailed from the 30s. Elvis discovered it on the flipside of Lavern Baker's 'Tweedle Dee', a song which he often performed onstage in the mid-Fifties. For release a decade later, RCA overdubbed the song with Nashville Sound musicians, but couldn't mask the haunting quality of Elvis's vocal. The undubbed original was eventually issued in the mid-Eighties.

Also rescued from the Fifties were two

songs taped for RCA – Billy Emerson's 'When It Rains, It Really Pours', another song Elvis had first tackled at Sun, and Hank Williams' 'Your Cheatin' Heart'. Not surprisingly, they outclassed the mish-mash of movie out-takes and studio leftovers that filled the rest of the album. Fans of Elvis's gentlest ballads would have taken heart from 'In My Way' (originally recorded for *Wild In The Country*, as was 'Forget Me Never') and the 1961 cut, 'I Met Her Today'. The rest, though, was pleasant but unmemorable.

Though all these songs are available on CD, this album line-up isn't.

HOW GREAT THOU ART (1967)

RCA began 1966 by releasing two successive singles from the 1960 LP, 'His Hand In Mine', neither of which charted. They ended it in possession of one of Elvis's finest sets of recordings, from which they were able to compile his second pure gospel album, 'How Great Thou Art'. Relishing the freedom of his first non-movie recording session in more than two

years, Elvis in June 1966 cut the 'Love Letters' single, the remarkable bonus tracks for the 'Spinout' soundtrack LP, and a great gospel album, which won Elvis a Grammy Award the following year.

The LP followed the format of 'His Hand In Mine', incorporated gospel chestnuts like 'Farther Along' and the title track as well as newer material. This time, though, Elvis added The Imperials gospel quartet and four female singers to the ensemble, creating a rich vocal tapestry that testified to the sincerity of his motives. To boost the album's commercial chances, RCA added the solitary out-take to have emerged from the 1960 gospel sessions — the hit single, 'Crying In The Chapel'.

The first CD release of this album mistakenly appeared in mono, though this was corrected on later copies.

THE COMPILATIONS

32 FILM HITS VOLS.1&2 (1985)

By careful dint of omitting anything that might cause too much embarrassment, these budget CD collections almost succeeded in rewriting history, by persuading buyers that Elvis's film career wasn't so disastrous after all. The first volume, in particular, was heavy on film-based singles and Fifties rockers, making it one of the more imaginative compilations on the market. After a diet that included 'Trouble', 'King Creole', 'Little Egypt' and 'Return To Sender', it was easy to overlook 'A Dog's Life' or 'Frankfurt Special' as an aberration.

The second volume had less to play with, and quickly ran into problems when it had to round up dubious suspects like 'Moonlight Swim', 'Island Of Love' and 'Relax'. But 'Jailhouse Rock' and 'Baby I Don't Care' were there to prove that not all the movie years were bad ones.

Until the complete film soundtracks are available on CD, these two double-disc collections are a useful introduction to the genre, with surprisingly good sound quality.

THE ELVIS PRESLEY COLLECTION VOLUME 3 (1986)

After two volumes covering the Fifties, the third of these basic hits CDs contin-

ued the story from 1960 to 1967.

The version of 'Follow That Dream' here is different from the original release; otherwise, the tracks are available in better shape elsewhere.

DIAMOND SERIES: ELVIS PRESLEY (1988)

Elvis's entry in a budget CD range offered a strange mix of Sixties material – everything from the sublime ('Tomorrow Is A Long Time') to the tiresome ('Do The Clam'), via some of the biggest hits from the period.

Beware of the lousy mastering job on this CD, which chops the beginnings off several songs. Cheap, but nasty.

FOR THE ASKING: THE LOST ALBUM (1990)

Lost but not missing: the contents of this album had all been issued in the Sixties, albeit never on the same package. Recognising that Elvis's first four studio LPs of that decade had all been assembled from purpose-built sessions, RCA set about creating a 'new' album from the studio outings of May 1963 and January 1964. Rather than spawning a follow-up to 'Pot Luck', these tracks had been spread across a baffling variety of singles and albums, with 'Devil In Disguise' becoming a Top 3 hit, 'Ask Me' narrowly missing the Top 10, and several other cuts surfacing on 'Elvis For Everyone' in 1965.

'For The Asking' was a neat idea, then, tastefully packaged in appropriate period artwork. But its role in the Elvis catalogue has effectively been annulled by the release of the 'From Nashville To Memphis' box set, which includes all this material and much more besides.

Another release conceived for the compact disc format.

FROM NASHVILLE TO MEMPHIS: THE ESSENTIAL 60'S MASTERS I (1993)

The second multi-CD box to emerge from Roger Semon and Ernst Mikael Jorgensen's trawl through the RCA archives not only restored to the catalogue many overlooked studio sessions;

it also went some way towards rehabilitating the least prestigious era of Elvis Presley's career.

Given the extent, and wide range in quality, of Elvis's Sixties recordings, RCA elected to separate his film work from his non-movie sessions. Going a stage further, this five-CD box also omits the gospel recordings, live material and tracks recorded for the NBC TV special, *Elvis*, in 1968. What's left is at least one version of every studio master Elvis recorded for secular, non-film releases between March 1960 and February 1969, plus a scattering of out-takes and rarities. Presented in sparkling stereo sound, and re-mastered from the best possible tapes, 'From Nashville To Memphis' is a six-hour voyage through choppy waters, ending in the safe haven of the Memphis sessions of 1969 (covered in more detail in the next section of this book).

With the film songs expunged, what's left is a remarkably hearty collection of pop material, that begins and ends with Elvis in peak form, and endures several decidedly dodgy periods along the way. What's remarkable, though, throughout the nine years of recordings, is the consistency of Presley's voice. Even when he sounds dispirited and marooned in a sea of strings or MOR arrangements, he never misses a note or throws away a single line. And when he's involved – whether it's singing the blues at the 'Elvis Is Back' sessions', or dragging together all his favourite genres at American Studios in Memphis nine years later – the power and flexibility of his voice is simply staggering.

The package is expertly annotated, lavishly illustrated, and full of discographical and biographical insight. Better still, it comes with a fistful of rarities, stretching from early, undubbed takes of late Sixties singles like 'In The Ghetto', 'Kentucky Rain' and 'Suspicious Minds' to the long-lost original 1963 recording of 'Memphis, Tennessee' – noticeably earthier than Presley's re-cut of the song a year later.

The versions of 'I'll Remember You', 'Hi-Heel Sneakers' and 'Guitar Man' run longer than any previous release – the last of these tracks revealing the extent of the segue into 'What'd I Say', first apparent on a 1980 release of the track. 'Big Boss Man', meanwhile, had almost a minute added to the 1967 single which signalled an about-turn in the downward path of Presley's recording career. Equally exciting is the alternate take of the 1961 single 'Surrender', cut before Elvis had hit upon the high-note ending familiar from the released version.

There's an unissued medley of 'This Time' and 'I Can't Stop Loving You' from the 1969 sessions; and, to close the set, an even more bizarre mingling of songs, on the 'Witchcraft'/'Love Me Tender' duets with Frank Sinatra from the first TV appearance Elvis made after returning from the Army. As with the 'Fifties Masters' set recommended elsewhere, 'From Nashville To Memphis' is essential listening.

Designed for CD, but also available on cassette and (in a limited edition) on vinyl.

The Comeback

In retrospect, history always seems inevitable. What could be more obvious than for Elvis to end the Sixties the way he began it, as the most prestigious live performer in America? Who better to return to his rock'n'roll roots in a year which saw a nostalgic surge of interest in the original Fifties rockers? And who else could have filled the void left by the demise of The Beatles in 1969?

What Presley fans always call 'the comeback' was a glorious two-year cycle of events, that began with the introduction of Jerry Reed to Elvis's sessions at the end of 1967, included the legendary *Elvis* TV special from 1968, encompassed the remarkable sessions at American Studios in Memphis, early in 1969, and culminated in the King reclaiming his throne in Las Vegas a few months later.

Yet events could easily have been different. Jerry Reed's presence at the session where Elvis recorded his great song, 'Guitar Man', nearly ended in farce, when Reed quite rightly refused to sign over the publishing royalties for the song to one of Presley's companies. Weaker songs had been discarded for less.

Then the TV special: the moment which persuaded the world that inside the sweet and inoffensive chest of Elvis Presley, lightweight film star, there still lurked the heart of a leather-clad rock'n'roller. The special was supposed to pull Elvis's career around, but if Colonel Parker's original plan had been adhered to, Elvis would have stepped before the cameras, delivered a saccharin selection of Christmas carols, and then retired gracefully to his den – much richer, but with the last vestiges of his reputation as the wildest rocker of the Fifties in flames.

So the comeback depended on luck as much as determination. One thing is certain, though. Between 1967 and 1969, Elvis cut his best records since the Fifties. Some rate them even higher than that; and few would argue that 1969 was the last golden year of his recording career. After American Studios, Elvis made some wonderful records, but none of them burned with the significance that he brought to those Memphis sessions.

What happened in those two years was that Elvis felt his way back towards the heart of his music. As a rocker in the Fifties, marrying the blues and country traditions with the rebellion of youth, Elvis sang the way he felt. Even his essentially conservative personality was catered for, via the gospel tunes, the Christmas carols and the romantic ballads.

Through the Sixties, Elvis's music, especially in Hollywood, bore no relation to anything that existed outside the movies. It took no notice of the changing world of pop, and made no attempt to satisfy Elvis's creative instincts. Vacuous and often inane, the film songs were simply means to an end, each epheremal ditty advancing the plot of another stupid movie, and hastening the end of his career as an important musical figure.

By the end of 1969, Elvis could look back on two years in which he had, to reheat a tired cliché, brought it all back home again. He returned to the black music and the country ballads that had always inspired him; he'd sung lyrics that tackled adult emotions rather than Hollywood fakery; he'd returned to his second home, the concert stage; and he'd remade his career in his own dream image. By the end of '69, the movies were over, and an apparently limitless future stretched in front of him. And if things didn't quite work out that way, then there was always the glory of '69 to remember.

THE ELVIS TV SPECIAL

The camera focused on a slim, lithe figure, clad in a body-hugging black leather suit, his hair a carefree mop of dark arrogance. "If you're looking for trouble," he sneered, "you've come to the right place."

It was a ten-year-old song, a refugee from the *King Creole* movie, and Elvis was the best part of a decade past his commercial prime. But for anyone who grew up with Elvis as a rock'n'roll icon, and for millions since who've thought themselves back into the mind-set of the times, it was an electrifying moment, an almost Christ-like return. The man they'd written off as dead, the breath squeezed out of his body by movie after stultifying movie, was suddenly reborn before their eyes – every bit as potent a sexual symbol as he'd been a decade earlier, but carrying the weight of years of disappointed dreams.

"He sang as if his life depended on it" is another cliché wheeled out on these occasions, but for once the hackneyed phrase rings true. Elvis could have carried on living if his TV special had failed – ironically, he might even have enjoyed a longer lifespan – but his career would effectively have been over. There was no chance of a second act in this performance: either Elvis matched his audience's expectations, or else in the year of the Paris uprising and the deaths of Robert Kennedy and Martin Luther King, he was consigned to history as the plaything of an outmoded generation.

Instead, he triumphed. Watched dispassionately, the TV special was nothing revolutionary. Elvis waltzed through a couple of production numbers, sang some gospel, sat in a boxing ring with some old friends and vamped through his early hits. The show closed with a production number calling for universal tolerance and peace. Big deal.

What mattered was what Elvis stood for. Having scattered his musical soul to the winds for an entire decade, Elvis finally reclaimed his past – and his audience's past as well. He returned to rock'n'roll for the first time since 1960. He performed as if he remembered why he'd ever wanted to be a singer in the first place. He mattered, in a way he hadn't since he'd cut 'Elvis Is Back!' eight years earlier.

Even on the rather erratic, mono-only

album of the event, titled 'Elvis: NBC TV Special', the significance of the occasion was preserved. True, the production number which saw Elvis segueing 'Guitar Man', 'Nothingville', 'Big Boss Man', 'Trouble' and 'Little Egypt' into one contrived sequence didn't work so well without the visuals. Stripped of the visual power of the leather-clad Presley wielding an electric guitar in anger for the first time since 1958, even the impromptu 'boxing ring' renditions of Sun classics and vintage blues songs lost a little of their lustre. But there was no doubting the power and passion of the voice.

On album and on a single issued to coincide with the TV screening, one performance stood out. Director Steve Binder, the man who'd countermanded Colonel Parker's original insistence that the show should feature Presley singing nothing more lethal than carols and hymns, made sure that Elvis heard a song written by the musical director for the programme, Earl Brown. That song was 'If I Can Dream', a heartfelt ballad with a keen, if unspecific, social message. Elvis fell for it immediately,

and agreed that the song should close the show.

Even without the pictures, 'If I Can Dream' sounded as if it was being delivered by a man dragging deep into his soul, exposing emotions he'd buried for years. On TV, it was apparent how much the song meant to Elvis – and how much it took out of him. For once, his vintage rock'n'roll gyrations weren't equal to the moment. Instead, the white-suited singer swung his free hand back and forth, in a gesture that suggested he was about to throw off some chains. As he reached the song's climax, he almost screeched the final notes. Then his face froze and he caught his breath in disbelief at what he'd done, before letting out a sigh that seemed half relief, half terror at how close he'd come to the edge. For those three minutes alone, the *Elvis* special deserves its place in history.

The majesty of the moment survived just long enough for the TV show to reach the world, and then dissolved into marketing. A week or two before the special aired, Singer (the company who'd sponsored it) issued an album with the rather sprawling title, 'Singer Presents Elvis Singing Flaming Star And Others'. The 'Others' included several movie leftovers, and one track from the special – a raw version of 'Tiger Man', first recorded for Sun by Rufus Thomas back in 1953. When the special was repeated in 1969, this performance replaced the seasonal 'Blue Christmas'.

On 1974's 'A Legendary Performer Vol. 1', RCA slipped out three further songs from the 'boxing ring': 'Trying To Get To You', 'Love Me' and 'Are You Lonesome Tonight'. The second LP in the series offered more: 'Blue Suede Shoes' and 'Baby What Do You Want Me To Do'. 'Vol. 3' in 1978 gave us 'Let Yourself Go' and 'It Hurts Me' from the studio sets that spawned the production numbers. The soundtrack to the documentary movie, *This Is Elvis*, produced yet another out-take: 'Blue Suede Shoes', spliced together from two separate versions of the song. And the fourth 'Legendary Performer' LP included a previously unheard version of 'That's All Right'.

Since then, both an extended version of the full TV special, and an uncut 'boxing ring' show, have been released on video. Finally, the original 'Elvis' LP has now been released on CD – with eight bonus cuts in all, rounding up the tracks which have been eked out over the years, and adding yet another out-take, 'Don't Be Cruel'.

Essential listening, even allowing for the variations in sound quality on the original recordings.

THE MEMPHIS SESSIONS

The success and (relative) daring of the *Elvis* special, combined with the decreasing audience for the movies, broke the mould of Presley's career. It was almost as if Elvis had forgotten what it was like to breathe, and having been reminded, was determined to cling to life regardless.

By the end of 1969, the old ways were gone for good, and at that stage their replacements had yet to become a strait-jacket. That year saw Elvis abandoning his acting career and returning to live performance. More importantly, he finally matured as a recording artist. The venue, appropriately enough, was a rundown studio in his adopted hometown of Memphis. American Sound Studio was run by producer Chips Moman, who in January 1969 was riding high on a series of blue-eyed soul hits that mixed elements of American roots music into the pop mainstream. Unlike RCA's company man, Felton Jarvis, Moman didn't work to anyone's authority but his own. Both RCA and Colonel Parker were horrified at the idea of an outsider dabbling with their prize artist, but Moman treated Elvis the way he had Dusty Springfield, The Box Tops and the rest. He found the songs, chose a reliable team of sessionmen, and created the most productive atmosphere possible for work to commence.

As Peter Guralnick's notes in the 'From Nashville To Memphis' box reveal, the Memphis sessions were more fraught than the legend allows. Elvis's managerial staff hassled songwriters over copyrights, and Elvis himself reacted angrily to Moman's occasionally heavy-handed studio methods. But you can't argue with the

results. During two weeks of sessions at American Sound, Chips Moman produced more great Elvis records than RCA's staff had managed over the previous five years. What's more, they were relevant to 1969 – not acid-rock freakouts, perhaps, but adult, soul-flavoured pop that didn't make Presley sound like an ageing uncle in a teenage world.

In view of the critical enthusiasm that's been bestowed upon the Memphis recordings over the years it's important to keep things in perspective. Between 1954 and 1956, Elvis changed the world. In 1969, he simply changed himself. But the first revolution came far more easily to him than the second. In the Fifties, he was doing what came naturally. In Memphis, he was fighting the advice of the entourage he'd trusted implicitly for more than a decade. The measure of what it cost him is that once he'd braved the new world, he retreated almost immediately. After 1971, he recorded in the studio only under extreme duress.

Elvis may never have returned to Chips Moman and American Sound after

February 1969, but the lessons he learned there weren't forgotten. Never again would he record juvenile pastiches of rock'n'roll, cobbled together by hack writers who had no interest in the genre. Even at their most hackneyed, the songs he recorded in the final eight years of his life had some relevance to Elvis himself – especially after his separation from his wife Priscilla, when he became a sucker for any song with a maudlin tune and a plot that ended with love betrayed.

Equally important was the realisation that the soul, blues and country which he adored could replace the crass pop he'd been handed for the previous decade. In particular, the Memphis sessions turned Elvis back into a country singer, albeit always with a tinge of Southern soul. Both styles had been systematically expunged from his music after 1960. Now they were making a long overdue reappearance.

THE SINGLES

Just four 45s emerged from the Moman sessions; but the first two, at least, were among the best ten records he ever made. It was Mac Davis who provided Elvis with 'In The Ghetto', a grim piece of social commentary which continued the theme of 'If I Can Dream', and came as close to protest singing as anything Presley ever recorded. Constructed around a tight, tense guitar line, it pushed Elvis into an emotional response.

Even better was Mark James' 'Suspicious Minds', which in Moman's hands became a brilliant soul record. An eternal tale of paranoia and deceit, it evidently struck a chord with Elvis, who heightened the tension of the verses, and then poured out his heart in the middle eight like a male Aretha Franklin. With the female backing singers urging him on, Elvis took the song right the way through to its brooding climax.

'Don't Cry Daddy' and 'Kentucky Rain' weren't quite in that league, but these two duets with country singer Ronnie Milsap (unbilled, of course: these *were* Elvis records) were still equal to any adult pop around. 'Kentucky Rain' was a dramatic portrayal of a man who didn't belong, and Elvis quickly identified with the story. It took him longer to grow into 'Don't Cry Daddy', but by the time he'd become estranged from Priscilla, the song had become one of his favourites.

FROM ELVIS IN MEMPHIS (1969)

Elvis's best album? It could be. It's certainly his best self-contained LP – i.e. not one that was concocted out of singles and leftovers, like his début way back in 1956. The album ended with 'In The Ghetto', but for once the single was purely incidental. It may have been one of Elvis's best ever 45s, but there are several cuts on the LP that outclass it.

One was 'Any Day Now', a thrilling re-interpretation of the early Sixties Chuck Jackson hit. This was great soul music, pure and simple, with Elvis's voice soaring free at one moment, biting down hard on a syllable the next. There was a liberation in his voice that had never been heard before, not even at Sun or in the TV special, combined with a maturity of phrasing that suggested he'd already

lived every nuance of the song.

'Long Black Limousine' made even that performance sound slight. It opened with the tolling of a funeral bell, before Elvis began to tell the story of a woman who'd left poverty, flirted with the dark temptation of wealth, and paid the ultimate price. Related that starkly, it sounds melodramatic, but Elvis's stunningly intense vocal gave it the unforgettable ring of a Biblical parable. As he reaches the moment of tragedy, his voice almost cracks with despair: reliving the victim's death, he seems to anticipate his own.

Those were the pivotal moments of the album, but everywhere you listened, Elvis was in total command. There was 'Power Of My Love', with Presley licking his lips lasciviously as he hadn't done since he'd left Sun. 'After Loving You' turned a simple blues tunes into an epic. 'It Keeps Right On A-Hurtin'' and 'I'll Hold You In My Heart' were slow, mournful country tunes that oozed emotional commitment. Even the relative throwaways, like a gallop through Hank Snow's 'I'm Movin' On', and the playful opener, 'Wearing

That Loved-On Look', made almost everything he'd recorded in the Sixties sound tame. For the duration of the album, Elvis sang as if he felt he was the greatest soul singer on the planet. His utter relief at being liberated from the movie treadmill is obvious on every track.

Available in isolation on CD, as well as (in part) on 'The Memphis Record', 'From Elvis In Memphis' is probably heard to best advantage as part of the 'From Nashville To Memphis' box.

BACK IN MEMPHIS (1969)

The second album taken from the Chips Moman sessions was originally part of a double-LP set, 'From Memphis To Vegas, From Vegas To Memphis', along with 'In Person At The International Hotel' (see Section 6). The latter was Elvis's first live album, and an event in itself. The publicity helped disguise the fact that 'Back In Memphis' was essentially the second-best of the American Sound sessions, the pick having already featured on 'From Elvis In Memphis' and various singles.

Not that it was a bad album. In fact, if the first Moman LP didn't exist, the Memphis sessions would still count as a triumph, on this evidence alone. There was nothing as breathtaking as 'Long Black Limousine', it's true, and occasionally the material threatened to define the word 'adult' as 'dull'. But the singing was, once again, superb.

The ironically titled 'Stranger In My Own Home Town', taken from an early Sixties soul record by Percy Mayfield, picked up the 'Any Day Now' award for emotional involvement, while 'And The Grass Won't Pay Any Mind' and 'Inherit The Wind' were assured, mature performances. Even the rather hackneyed revival of Ned Miller's country hit, 'From A Jack To A King', swaggered with self-confidence.

The rest of the record was low-key but always enjoyable – a more subtle collection than 'From Elvis In Memphis', but a less memorable one. In an ideal world, of course, Elvis would have left several of these tracks on the shelf, and gone back to Chips Moman for another session. In the real world, we should be thankful for every Memphis track we get.

As above: you're probably better off with the boxed set than with the CD version of this LP, or 'The Memphis Record'.

THE MEMPHIS RECORD (1987)

This should have been the killer. Across two albums, RCA repackaged 23 of the 29 Chips Moman recordings, omitting the one dog from the sessions – 'Hey Jude'.

Sadly, someone had the bright idea of remixing the tracks, with the result that much of their power is lost. It doesn't sound dreadful, but it doesn't sound right, either. For the complete Memphis recordings, go instead to the 'From Nashville To Memphis' box set discussed earlier.

The CD and LP versions of this set are identical.

The Final Years 5

In 1968 and 1969, Elvis made the finest records of his career. His return to live performance provoked rave reviews; his was the hottest ticket in show business. In 1970 and 1971, he toured, recorded and racked up hit records all over the world. In 1977, he died – addicted to prescription drugs, bloated and beached, his talents in shreds, bent out of shape by years on the road, and not having seen the inside of a professional recording studio in more than two years. In the words of a book that appeared just before his death: Elvis, what happened?

The straight answer is that Elvis squandered his talent, and his physical and emotional resources. In his dealings with Colonel Parker, Elvis abhorred conflict. Only on one occasion – when the 1968 TV special was being conceived – do we hear of Elvis going against the Colonel's wishes. When the management organisation wanted Elvis to make movies, he made movies, and threw away the years which could have been his artistic peak. When they told him to tour, he toured, while the benefits of his hard-won 'comeback' at the end of the Sixties seeped away.

Racked by constant ill-health, which was half provoked, half checked by his regular input of pills, Elvis dragged his body out on the road, month after month. He'd grown to need the sound of the audience's cry, and some part of him preferred the safety of reviving his vintage hits, night after night, to the danger of trying to create some new ones.

But his refusal to record after 1971 is impossible to explain away. Worn down by his work schedule, he may have regarded RCA's demands for new product as one pressure too many. But given his obvious delight in the studio between late 1967 and the summer of 1971, his sudden withdrawal from recording thereafter takes on an almost suicidal air.

After a flurry of first-rate material at the start of the Seventies, RCA were forced to concoct albums out of leftovers, live cuts, and a continuous stream of showcase concerts. By 1975, they were reduced to bringing the studio to Elvis, setting up shop at his Memphis home, Graceland, where at least they could be sure that Elvis had not yet left the building. Eventually, even that tactic failed. When Presley died, on the verge of another exhausting tour, RCA were at their wits' end. The cynical comment that his death was a good career move wasn't so far from the truth.

THE SINGLES

Even the titles of Elvis's Seventies singles seem to chart the course of his decline – from 'The Wonder Of You' to 'Moody

Blue' and 'Way Down'. But perhaps the most prophetic title was 'I've Lost You'. The most significant event in Elvis's final seven years was the collapse of his marriage to Priscilla Beaulieu. The couple had met when Elvis had been serving in Germany in the late Fifties – Priscilla then barely into her teens. She moved to Memphis to be with him in the Sixties, but they weren't finally married until 1968. After their decade-long courtship, their union lasted little more than three years, before Priscilla exchanged the King for his karate teacher. The couple shared the upbringing of their daughter, Lisa Marie, and kept in relatively close contact for her sake. But despite Elvis's strong relationships with at least two other women in his final years, he seems never to have fully recovered from Priscilla's departure.

For perhaps the only time in his life, Elvis began to use his music as a form of autobiography. Between 1972 and 1976, he recorded a disproportionate number of lachrymose, sometimes desolate country songs, which documented the loss of true love. While these songs made his albums painful listening, they often worked well as singles. His last release of 1972 coupled 'Separate Ways' with 'Always On My Mind', Elvis singing both numbers entirely from the heart. 'Fool' from 1973 fitted the same category, while 'My Boy' took a fictional look at his own situation. And there were countless more examples on albums from 'Elvis' (1973) to 'From Elvis Presley Boulevard' (1976).

Before then, Elvis had been perfecting a genre which you could call 'the Las Vegas ballad'. Epic in scope, as befitted the world's greatest entertainer, they called for huge orchestrations, and an equally huge vocal. Elvis developed the style to cope, sometimes veering close to breast-beating self-parody, but usually carrying all before him as he boomed out across the Vegas strings and horns. His revival of the Fifties hit 'The Wonder Of You' inaugurated the trend, which was continued by a succession of remakes of other artists' hits, like 'You Don't Have To Say You Love Me' (Dusty Springfield), 'There Goes My Everything' (Engelbert Humperdinck) and 'Rags To Riches' (a

gargantuan performance of a song made famous by Tony Bennett).

After the gospel song 'Life', which wasn't expected to be a Top 40 hit, Elvis issued 'I'm Leavin' ', a return to the sound of his Memphis sessions. Neither that single nor its follow-up, the equally intriguing 'It's Only Love', made the US Top 30; and while Elvis continued to find success in Britain, 'Until It's Time For You To Go' and (incredibly) 'An American Trilogy' made an even more disappointing showing on the US charts. The record that transformed Elvis's commercial slide was 'Burning Love', his first authentic rock'n'roll single since 'Guitar Man' at the end of 1967. Built around a tense rhythm that was always on the verge of bubbling over, 'Burning Love' reminded the world why Elvis had been called the King of Rock'n'Roll. The single went all the way to No. 2, his biggest hit since the equally powerful 'Suspicious Minds' in 1973.

Then came the separation, killing off hopes of a rock revival. 'Raised On Rock' in 1973 was a good title, but a clichéd, mid-pace song. Then, another miracle:

the end of the rock'n'roll revival. For his final singles, Elvis reverted to country ('Bringing It Back' and the upbeat 'Moody Blue'), a staggering bellow through the Timi Yuro oldie 'Hurt', and then a rather lame semi-disco rock pastiche called 'Way Down' – which would have been forgotten in weeks if it hadn't been on the charts when Presley died. Instead, it became his first British No. 1 since 1970.

STUDIO ALBUMS 1970-1977

THAT'S THE WAY IT IS (1970)

The soundtrack album to the brilliant documentary, *Elvis – That's The Way It Is*. Not exactly. The album was released alongside the movie, and contained many of the songs heard in the film, but only two performances heard on celluloid made it onto the record. Like many of Elvis's Seventies albums, 'That's The Way It Is' was a collage of live and studio recordings. In one case, 'Bridge Over Troubled Water', the collage extended as far as a single track, with a studio version

after the soul-flavoured 'I've Got A Thing About You Baby' and the brooding 'If You Talk In Your Sleep', another rock classic, as Elvis tackled Chuck Berry's standard, 'Promised Land'. It sounded as if it had been taped during a studio jam, but it hit as hard as anything he'd cut since he left the Army.

'My Boy' was followed by 'T-R-O-U-B-L-E' – another full-tilt performance of a song that may have been contrived, but rocked like hell as compensation. But that was of the song edited onto the final chord of a live rendition, which was unfortunately in a different key.

That one slip aside, 'That's The Way It Is' was a worthy successor to Elvis's previous studio set, 'Back In Memphis'. With Chips Moman's studios having gone bankrupt, Elvis returned to the familiar environs of RCA at Nashville, with Felton Jarvis back in command. Across five days of sessions in June 1970, Elvis recorded more than 30 songs – enough for three albums and any number of spin-off singles. Country-flavoured material was saved for another project, but the best of the rest ended up on this album.

Among the highlights of the record were a commanding reading of the ballad 'How The Web Was Woven', previously recorded by British singer Jackie Lomax; a subtle version of 'Mary In The Morning', formerly a hit for Al Martino; and an attractive pop song called 'The Next Step Is Love' (satirised by Elvis as 'The Next Step Is Sex' in the movie).

Alongside these studio cuts were powerful live versions of The Righteous Brothers' 'You've Lost That Lovin' Feelin' ', a soul-tinged rocker called 'Patch It Up' (also recorded for single release during the studio session) and, best of all, a beautiful 'I Just Can't Help Believing', a B.J. Thomas hit which Elvis made his own.

The authority of Presley's singing helped disguise the fact that the album stepped decisively away from the American-roots inspiration of the Memphis sessions towards a more middle-of-the-road sound. With country put on the backburner, and soul and R&B left in Memphis, what was left was very classy, very clean white pop – perfect for the Las Vegas crowd, but a definite retrograde step for Elvis.

ELVIS COUNTRY (1971)

A concept album? Yes indeed. Given the Nashville setting and orientation of his music over the last decade, it was surprising that RCA hadn't hit on this idea before. One new song aside, this was a collection of country standards, occasionally veering towards the outer reaches of rockabilly, which allowed Elvis to turn in warm, affectionate readings of songs that he loved.

With a picture of the two-year-old Elvis on the cover, emphasising his rural origins, and the linking device of a country-rock tune called 'I Was Born About 10,000 Years Ago' inserted between each track, 'Elvis Country' took on a unity that was welcomed by fans and critics alike. Occasionally, the album strayed a little towards blandness, as on the opening cover of Anne Murray's recent hit, 'Snowbird'. But elsewhere, there was no doubting Elvis's commitment to the music, whether it was on a stately stroll through Willie Nelson's 'Funny How Time Slips Away', or a more energetic version of the Jerry Lee Lewis rock hit, 'Whole Lotta Shakin' Goin' On'. 'Little Cabin On The Hill' stressed Elvis's love of bluegrass, while 'The Fool' (a version of the Fifties hit by Sanford Clark) turned the wheel full circle, by covering a song that had originally been recorded in the Presley style.

The album spawned one single, with the coupling of 'I Really Don't Want To Know' and 'There Goes My Everything', and it proved the strength of those June 1970 sessions in Nashville – all but two of the songs having been recorded then. The exceptions were 'Whole Lotta Shakin' Goin' On' and 'Snowbird', both of which came from a return visit in September, which also provided the minor hit single, 'Rags To Riches'. For the moment, at least, Elvis fans could assure themselves that their man was still in peak form.

LOVE LETTERS FROM ELVIS (1971)

In its packaging, concept and contents, 'Love Letters From Elvis' – the third new album in six months – was an unfortunate return to the cynical ways of the past. Despite the photos of a reasonably sleek, jump-suited Elvis on stage in Vegas, the album was yet another trawl through the June 1970 Nashville sessions. As a third bite at an increasingly tired cherry, it was not surprisingly a rather lacklustre collection.

It's not clear why Elvis chose to re-record

his 1966 hit single, 'Love Letters', in an arrangement that was virtually identical to the original. All he brought to this second attempt was his deeper, more 'mature' vocal style; otherwise, this remake lacked the lightness of touch heard on the original. On an album distressingly short on highlights, though, 'Love Letters' still stood out. The ballad-orientated set reached its nadir with the British song 'This Is Our Dance', which would have been ideal for Engelbert Humperdinck but insulted the reputation of the former King of Rock'n'Roll. Two gospel numbers, 'Only Believe' and 'Life', quickened the tempo but not the pulse. A succession of maudlin, country-tinged songs were passable in isolation, but deadening in succession. Aside from a hearty romp through 'Heart Of Rome', another song of British origin which was slipped onto the flipside of Elvis's next single, the album had only one saving grace – and that came almost by accident.

During a break in the Nashville sessions, Elvis and the band drifted into an impromptu medley of Muddy Waters' blues standard, 'Got My Mojo Working', and Damita Jo's 1961 hit, 'Keep Your Hands Off Her'. Recorded for fun rather than money, 'Got My Mojo Working' was duly overdubbed with vocals and extra instruments, and tossed onto the 'Love Letters' album, where it easily outclassed all its neighbours. It said something about the prevailing atmosphere of the project that Muddy Waters' song was credited to one 'Preston Foster' instead.

Strangely, this was the first of the Seventies studio albums to be issued on compact disc.

ELVIS SINGS THE WONDERFUL WORLD OF CHRISTMAS (1971)

As 'Love Letters From Elvis' reached the shops in May 1971, Elvis was hard at work in RCA Studios in Nashville – recording a Christmas album. Legend has it that the studio was decorated with Christmas beads and baubles to get the participants in a festive mood, but you couldn't deduce that from the record. On a mixture of hymns and lightweight pop material, Elvis never came close to getting involved in the subject or the songs. The results were predictably tasteful and lacking in emotion – perfect for a seasonal album from a performer who was learning once again to put cash before commitment.

Just to annoy or entice the fans, the 'Wonderful World Of Christmas' LP had one track which broke out of the stiflingly anodyne mood. Like 'Got My Mojo Working' on the previous album, the Charles Brown blues hit 'Merry Christmas Baby' started out as a studio jam, which was edited into shape for the album. You can tell from the ad-libs that Elvis never figured this lazy, simmering R&B tune would be released – which is precisely why it's more relaxed, soulful and enjoyable than anything else on the record. Issued in a slightly longer version after Elvis's death, it became a UK hit, and was finally acknowledged as one of the best performances of his later years. Like most of its rivals for that position, it was only captured on tape by chance.

The compact disc release of this album

features the long 'Merry Christmas Baby', an alternative version of 'I'll Be Home On Christmas Day', and a one-off seasonal single from 1966, 'If Every Day Was Like Christmas'.

ELVIS NOW (1972)

As early as 1971, Presley seems to have regarded recording sessions as a chore rather than a pleasure. The result was albums like this one, a jigsaw puzzle of out-takes from various studio engagements which didn't quite fit together. Any album which featured the worst leftovers from the 1969 Memphis sessions ('Hey Jude') and the June 1970 dates in Nashville ('Sylvia') didn't have much going for it. Add in the repetition (the full-length 'I Was Born About 10,000 Years Ago', last heard in pieces on 'Elvis Country') and the tired (makeweight interpretations of 'Early Morning Rain' and 'Help Me Make It Through The Night'), and 'Elvis Now' was fast regressing to the standards of the mid-Sixties.

Only one song sounded as if it had aroused Elvis's artistic interest. 'Until It's

Time For You To Go' had been written and first recorded by Buffy Sainte-Marie, but it's more likely that Elvis had heard the version by one of his favourite singers of this period, Neil Diamond. His rendition lacked the emotional drama and orchestral bluster of his best 1970 and 1971 recordings, but Elvis at least sang the lyrics as if he'd read them before the start of the session. That aside, the album lived up to its title in the worst possible sense. No wonder that RCA started interleaving live albums with the increasingly mediocre studio collections.

HE TOUCHED ME (1972)

Elvis won a Grammy for his third and final new collection of spiritual songs, though by common consent this was the weakest of the set. How could it be anything else when it was recorded during the same uninvolved sessions as the second Christmas album, and some of the weaker tracks on 'Elvis Now'?

 The tried and trusted Imperials gospel quartet tried their best to invest tunes like 'I, John' with some born-again fervour,

but once the pace slackened, everyone from Elvis down began to sound bored, not uplifted. But the material did at least have the advantage of melodic and lyrical inspiration, something that wasn't the case with the worst of the new songs Elvis recorded in 1971.

 What's missing from the album, ultimately, is any feeling that it needed to be made. Like the Christmas LP, it was a marketing exercise, to help Elvis cover all the commercial bases. The trouble was, both albums gave the game away far too easily.

Issued in full on CD.

ELVIS (1973)

Between June 1971 and July 1973, Elvis held just one studio session – the spring 1972 date which spawned two hit singles, 'Separate Ways'/'Always On My Mind' and the mighty 'Burning Love'. Unfortunately, July 1973 was also the month when RCA had scheduled the next Elvis studio LP. So there was no alternative but to revive the dead ducks from the 1971 sessions, alongside Elvis's latest single, the aptly titled 'Fool'.

RCA's original intention had been to fill half the 'Elvis' LP with Hawaiian songs taped after the 'Aloha From Hawaii' concert in January 1973. Also on that provisional running order was a tantalising item called 'A Blues Jam' – actually a version of the 'Elvis Is Back' classic 'Reconsider Baby', recorded at Madison Square Garden the previous June.

Instead, the Hawaii tracks and the blues jam were dropped. Songs like 'For Lovin' Me' and 'Padre' were rescued from the 1971 tape archive, and placed alongside a motley collection of tracks – three of which had supposedly been taped by Elvis alone at the piano, and subsequently overdubbed for release. Either way, they were depressingly maudlin.

As usual, the exception to the mediocrity was a jam session – this time the edited highlights of a lengthy work-out around the chords of Bob Dylan's 'Don't Think Twice, It's All Right'. Against that, a live-in-Las-Vegas crawl through Perry Como's hit, 'It's Impossible', wasn't much competition.

RAISED ON ROCK/FOR OL' TIMES SAKE (1973)

It should have been a classic: Elvis Presley, back in Memphis one more time, and teamed with the legendary house band at the city's premier soul shack, Stax Studios on McLemore Avenue. But Stax was only a few months away from bankruptcy, and the Elvis who'd committed himself wholeheartedly to the American Sound sessions in 1969 was four years down the pike. At Stax in July 1973, Presley bitched about the set-up, the equipment and the songs, and this album was only completed with the aid of a hastily-scheduled session at his home in Palm Springs, California, a few weeks later.

Even so, 'Raised On Rock/For Ol' Times Sake' should have been more inspired than it was. The album took its clumsy title from its lead-off single, which inauspiciously flopped. The A-side was written by Mark James of 'Suspicious Minds' fame, but that was all this clichéd 'history of rock' tune had going for it. Worse still,

Elvis's first new songs from the Jerry Leiber/Mike Stoller team in more than a decade weren't any more inspired.

When Elvis couldn't even fake up a storm on the old Rosco Gordon R&B hit, 'Just A Little Bit', times were rough indeed. His old pal, Jerry Lee Lewis, showed what could be done with the same tune at another Memphis session around the same time, but Elvis just didn't seem to care. Sadly, it's hard to avoid passing the same sentence on the whole album.

GOOD TIMES (1974)

Despite the uptempo revivalist vibe of 'Talk About The Good Times', the song from which the album took its title, this record suggested that Elvis realised the only good times around were in the past. The LP closed with Danny O'Keeffe's painfully apt 'Good Time Charlie's Got The Blues', which drew from Elvis one of the most impressive performances of his final years. The poignancy lies in the lyric, which conveys the emotional decline of a man who'd once made the party swing. Elvis sang it as if he'd already lived out all

those implications, and more besides.

Equally affecting was 'My Boy', a sentimental ballad in which a father tries to console his son, and himself, after a painful separation. You didn't need to be an analyst to work out the autobiographical impact the song had on Elvis: his vocal delivery said it all.

Not everything on this record, mostly cut in Palm Springs during the 'emergency' sessions of September 1973, was in that class. Elvis's renditions of 'She Wears My Ring' and 'Spanish Eyes' cruised into cabaret territory, while the vaguely disco ambience of 'I Got A Feelin' In My Body' was unconvincing. But the flexibility of the vocal on Tom Jans' ballad, 'Lovin' Arms', and Elvis's attempt to match the swamp-rock feel of 'I've Got A Thing About You Baby', intimated that the game wasn't up yet.

PROMISED LAND (1975)

Like 'Merry Christmas Baby', 'Got My Mojo Working' and 'Don't Think Twice, It's All Right', the title track of this album arose from an off-the-cuff jam session –

though this time Elvis and the band paused long enough to work up an arrangement. The young-American-made-good narrative of Chuck Berry's lyrical rocker was perfect for Elvis, regardless of his health and mood, and he steamed through the number like a greyhound off the leash.

For an album made up of the second choice of material from the Palm Springs session, 'Promised Land' was much more impressive than it had any right to be. Without threatening the idle course of Elvis's career, it contained a bunch of performances that sounded as if they'd been recorded and sung with care, rather than under contractual obligation. The steamy 'If You Talk In Your Sleep' had already made a convincing single, while country ballads like 'There's A Honky Tonk Angel', 'Love Song Of The Year' and 'It's Midnight' were less maudlin than recent offerings. 'You Asked Me To', written by Billy Joe Shaver, even threatened to take the King into Outlaw Country. Sadly, Elvis died before the champion of the duet singers, Willie Nelson, could get his hands on him. Their version of 'Night Life' might have been worth hearing.
Available on CD.

TODAY (1975)

Elvis's last professional studio session produced, suitably enough, his last great rocker. 'T-R-O-U-B-L-E', written by Jerry Chesnut, took the feel of 'Promised Land', turned up the tempo a notch, and provoked Elvis into one final display of Tupelo Mississippi Flash. So tarnished was the reputation of his recording career, though, that this near-classic barely scraped into the Top 40.

Sadly, it proved to be unrepresentative of the 'Today' album, which was at least a degree or two stronger than the equally revealing 'Elvis Now' a few years earlier. In Presley's 'Today' of March 1975, the prevailing mood was unoriginality – which was why the album revived others' hits, like The Pointer Sisters' 'Fairytale', Billy Swan's 'I Can Help' (painfully over-sung by Elvis), The Statler Brothers ('Susan When She Tried'), Perry Como ('And I Love You So') and, of course, Tom Jones

('Green Green Grass Of Home'). Most of Presley's performances were perfectly solid, but patently light on inspiration. It took the close-to-the-bone lyrics of Try Seals' song, 'Pieces Of My Life', to drag any genuine emotional commitment out of Elvis's singing.

Available on CD.

FROM ELVIS PRESLEY BOULE- VARD, MEMPHIS, TENNESSEE (1976)

"Recorded Live", boasted the cover on Elvis's final studio record – and so it was, though not in the Vegas-like surroundings that the phrase implied. Elvis proving impossible to entice into the studio, the studio came to Elvis: Felton Jarvis was forced to turn the den at Graceland into a recording complex, an operation made more tortuous by Presley's insistence that he, the musicians and the back-up singers should all be taped at the same time.

An additional blight on these sessions was Elvis's physical health. Overweight, over-strained, over-medicated and suffering from a variety of ailments more befitting a man twice his age, Elvis was in no state to record. But for a week, that's exactly what he did: the stress on his system is audible on every track. His voice had grown rounder – fruitier, even – with age: on this album, it sounded bloated and hollow, like a glass balloon about to shatter into a thousand fragments. Anyone with an ounce of empathy will find listening to this record a painful experience, but Elvis's determination to stay the course gives the entire enterprise a tragic grandeur.

Nowhere is that more pertinent than on 'Hurt', an epic battle between physical dissolution and artistic striving that ends in magnificent stalemate. Elvis had never made a ballad sound so big, or so deadly. Much of the album had the grim fascination of watching an overweight tightrope walker stumbling blindfold over a gaping ravine. But while he stayed on the wire, the results were impressive enough – whether it was a bluesy cruise through the country standard, 'Blue Eyes Crying In The Rain', or the King's doomed attempt to rock out on 'For The Heart'. But when the rope broke, the voice went with it, leaving 'I'll Never Fall In

'Love Again', to name but one, awash with missed notes and laboured breathing.

MOODY BLUE (1977)

After the sessions for 'Elvis Presley Boulevard', Elvis was able to attempt only one more set of recordings at home – and they spawned just four complete tracks. Another session was booked for February 1977, but Elvis cancelled it. Instead, RCA rushed out 'Welcome To My World', a collection of previously released country tunes, boosted by an otherwise unavailable live version of 'I Can't Stop Loving You'.

In June, there was a single – a mediocre rocker called 'Way Down'. A month later, an album followed, named after a minor 1976 hit, 'Moody Blue'. It scraped together the dregs of the '76 Graceland sessions, and added in a trio of live tracks from concerts in April 1977. Even that wasn't enough, and so RCA reprised 'Let Me Be There' from the Memphis live LP of 1974.

Two performances of country standards stood out, as both 'He'll Have To Go' and 'She Thinks I Still Care' were sung with some kind of involvement. In concert, as

ever, Elvis was still trying sporadically to impress, and his overblown 'Unchained Melody' was fairly impressive. But the rest sounded like the ragbag it was.

Elvis could scarcely have planned a less appropriate farewell; but four weeks after 'Moody Blue' reached the shops, its reluctant creator was dead. The album instantly went gold, 'Way Down' topped the British charts, and the twin process of canonisation and debunking began. Rarely have so many people bought so shoddy an album.

Available on CD, but not a recommended starting-point for any Elvis collection, even of Seventies studio albums.

SEVENTIES CD COMPILATIONS

ALWAYS ON MY MIND (1985)

With a remix of the title track for completists, and several album tracks unavailable elsewhere on CD, this maudlin collection of Elvis weepies from the late Sixties and Seventies confirms the way in which he used his music to convey the disintegrating state of his marriage.

Good CD sound quality on this set.

ELVIS — THE COLLECTION VOLUME FOUR (1986)

From 'Guitar Man' in 1967 to 'Always On My Mind' five years later, a representative but not complete singles collection. Often overlooked titles like 'Rags To Riches' and 'There Goes My Everything' are there, but the CD is docked a point or two for omitting 'I'm Leavin' '.

The sound quality is impressive, but several tracks are included in mono rather than stereo.

Elvis Live

Aside from his 1955 appearance in the movie *The Pied Piper Of Cleveland*, which has been lost in legal tangles since it was made, there is virtually no live footage of Elvis, Scotty and Bill in their prime. The same few seconds of silent film are wheeled out whenever Elvis's early years are under discussion: otherwise, documentary makers are restricted to the fictional live performances in movies like *Loving You* and *Jailhouse Rock*.

 A decade or more later, when Elvis returned to the road in Las Vegas, cameras were ready. Around a dozen Presley concerts were officially filmed over the final years of his life, and nearly as many

were documented on record. From documentary movies like *Elvis – That's The Way It Is* and *Elvis On Tour* comes our strongest visual memory of the man on stage, clad in outlandish jumpsuits, backed by a cabaret orchestra and rehearsing his karate moves to the pumped-up revivals of his vintage hits.

 During the Seventies, when Elvis developed a phobia for the studio, regular live recordings were RCA's lifeline. But it was only after his death that Presley's live career began to be represented on record. Despite legal complexities, a bunch of pre-RCA shows – mostly taped for the syndicated radio series, the

Louisiana Hayride – slipped onto the market. RCA followed by giving a legal release to a bootleg tape of a rare 1961 performance in Hawaii, alongside the sole evidence of Elvis's first attempt at conquering Las Vegas, way back in 1956.

It took the release of the 6-LP set 'A Golden Celebration' in 1984 to document the live phenomenon that was Elvis in the Fifties. Since then, there have been several additions to the canon – more Vegas shows, even an alternative version of the legendary Aloha From Hawaii show from early 1973. On CD, though, the representation of Elvis on stage is painfully thin – whether it's the Fifties or the Seventies that you regard as his golden era.

THE ROCK'N'ROLL YEARS

LOUISIANA HAYRIDE
(1954-1956)

Like the *Grand Ole Opry*, the *Louisiana Hayride* was a radio show syndicated across the Southern States every Saturday night. Broadcast out of Shreveport, Louisiana, it was aired on nearly 200 radio stations, and allowed millions of listeners to hear the latest country music stars in front of a live audience.

Elvis first played the *Hayride* two weeks after his sole, abortive appearance on the *Grand Ole Opry*. It was October 1954, and he was just another struggling country singer with two singles to his name. Over the next two years, he made an incredible 50 performances on the *Hayride* – one of which, in March 1955, was also broadcast live on TV in Shreveport.

Most of those *Hayride* shows are lost forever, but a handful have survived, and have been issued on albums like 'Elvis: The First Live Recordings' and 'The Hillbilly Cat'. They add covers of Lavern Baker's 'Tweedlee Dee' and Chuck Berry's 'Maybellene' to Elvis's known repertoire, but otherwise duplicate his early singles – though the live atmosphere adds a frisson of excitement that isn't spoiled by the poor recording quality. Those last two songs were also included on 'The Complete Fifties Masters'.

EAGLE'S HALL, HOUSTON, TEXAS (1955)

Issued briefly in the late Seventies as 'The First Year', five songs taped at one of Elvis's favourite pre-Sun haunts remain the only record of his appearances on another radio syndication, *Grand Prize Saturday Night Jamboree*. Four of the songs also appear on his Sun singles; the fifth, 'I Got A Woman', was recorded at RCA for his first album.

PRIME-TIME TV (1956-1957)

On January 28, 1956, Elvis made his first national TV appearance, as the guest of the Dorsey Brothers on CBS's *Stage Show*. Backed by Scotty, Bill, drummer D.J. Fontana and the out-of-place Dorsey Orchestra, Elvis segued two Joe Turner hits, 'Shake Rattle And Roll' and 'Flip Flop And Fly', and performed his dramatic rendition of Ray Charles' 'I Got A Woman'.

To an audience expecting light entertainment, Elvis's unashamedly sexual pelvic thrusts and full-throated roar were nothing short of a revolution. Elvis repeated the impression on five further editions of *Stage Show* in February and March, this time remembering to plug his single, 'Heartbreak Hotel', but also steaming through songs like 'Tutti Frutti', 'Baby Let's Play House' and 'Blue Suede Shoes'.

In early April, Elvis switched networks to NBC, where he taped four songs for the *Milton Berle Show*, in the unlikely surroundings of the dock of the *USS Hancock*, docked in San Diego. Without the distractions of an orchestra, the four rock'n'rollers scorched through 'Shake Rattle And Roll', 'Heartbreak Hotel' and 'Blue Suede Shoes' one more time. In June, Elvis guested with Berle again, this time in Hollywood – performing his latest release, 'I Want You, I Need You, I Love You' for the first time on TV, and previewing his next single, 'Hound Dog'.

Four weeks later, he played the same two songs on another NBC programme, *The Steve Allen Show*. Watched by a lugubrious hound perched on a stool and sporting a top hat, a tuxedoed Elvis managed to overcome the satire and the constraints that Allen had tried to place on his on-stage hip-swaying.

But it was Ed Sullivan, the host of CBS's *Toast of The Town*, who has gone into rock history as the man who insisted on filming Elvis solely from the waist up. Sullivan was absent the first night Elvis played his show, and Charles Laughton did the honours instead. After a second performance in October, Sullivan was inundated with complaints from viewers about the carnality of Presley's movements. On January 6, 1957, then, when Elvis was booked to perform no fewer than seven songs on *Toast Of The Town*, Sullivan's cameramen were under strict instructions to keep the infamous pelvis off the screen. And Elvis added a straight gospel rendition of 'Peace In The Valley' to prove he was a regular boy after all.

Taken together, these 12 TV appearances constitute Elvis's introduction to post-teen America – plus the first great clash between rock'n'roll and TV. After being available on bootlegs for years, all 12 were assembled in remarkable sound quality on the 1984 box set, 'A Golden Celebration', but as yet they have not been issued on CD.

NEW FRONTIER HOTEL, LAS VEGAS (May 1956)

Years before the white jumpsuits and 'Also Sprach Zarathustra', Elvis played in the Venus Room of one of Las Vegas's most prestigious hotels – and flopped. As you can hear from the recording of his final show on the 'Elvis Aron Presley' box set, audience reaction was lukewarm, the Freddie Martin Orchestra supplied an incongruous backing, and Elvis himself was embarrassingly gauche as a stand-up comedian.

The entire set – which includes what might be rock'n'roll's first-ever drum solo – was included on 'The Complete Fifties Masters'.

THE MISSISSIPPI-ALABAMA FAIR AND DAIRY SHOW (September 1956)

Also included on 'A Golden Celebration' was a remarkable recording of Elvis's appearance at the annual fair held in his hometown of Tupelo, Mississippi on September 26, 1956. Thirteen years earlier, Elvis had made his first public appearance at the event, winning second prize in the talent contest by singing 'Old Shep'. In 1956, by contrast, the organisers declared 'Elvis Presley Day' – and the honoree responded by playing afternoon and evening shows to an ecstatic crowd of locals, as well as helping out the organisers by making stage announcements and presentations to the winners of various contests at the fair.

More than any of the Presley live recordings from the Fifties, these two shows – chronicled in full on that 1984 box set – capture the mixture of naïve enthusiasm and sexual excitement which Elvis aroused from his audience. Sadly, though, these recordings remain unavailable on CD at the time of writing.

WELCOME HOME, ELVIS (May 1960)

After touring non-stop through 1955 and 1956, Elvis cut back his live appearances in 1957 to a mere 23 nights, at venues that ranged from a return visit to the Tupelo fairgrounds, to his only shows outside US territory, in Ottawa, Toronto and

at the Empire Stadium in Vancouver. Ten days after Elvis's only live dates of 1958, in Russwood Park, Memphis, he joined the Army. And three weeks after he was discharged, in March 1960, he taped a six-minute appearance on this TV show, sponsored by Timex and hosted by Frank Sinatra.

Intended by Colonel Parker as a deliberate effort to widen Elvis's audience, the show saw him perform both sides of his comeback single, 'Stuck On You', and then share a historic duet with Sinatra – Presley tackling Frank's hit, 'Witchcraft', and Sinatra reciprocating with 'Love Me Tender'. This bizarre event is captured on the 'From Nashville To Memphis' CD box set.

HAWAII BENEFIT SHOW (March 1961)

Elvis's first live shows in three years took place at the Ellis Auditorium in Memphis, on February 25, 1961. Exactly a month later came his last appearance for more than eight years – a charity concert, like the Memphis shows, at Bloch Arena,

Pearl Harbor, Hawaii. Elvis was in the most westerly US state to film *Blue Hawaii*, and his concert was staged to raise funds for the building of the *USS Arizona* memorial – in honour of the thousand or more sailors killed on that ship during the Pearl Harbor air attack of 1941. In theory, this should be the classic document of the early Elvis on stage, as it features the 'Elvis Is Back' band, and a fine repertoire of material that dips into that album as well as hit singles from 1954 to 1961. But the show only exists as an amateur recording, in painfully thin, trebly sound. RCA purchased the tape for the 'Elvis Aron Presley' box set in 1980, but have (perhaps sensibly) refrained from issuing it on CD.

THE CONCERT YEARS

THE ELVIS TV SPECIAL
(June 1968)

Full details of this initial comeback performance can be found in Section 4.

ELVIS IN PERSON AT THE INTERNATIONAL HOTEL, LAS VEGAS (1969)

Thirteen years after leaving Nevada's gambling paradise as a failure, Elvis returned to Las Vegas in triumph. The 2,000-seater showroom at the International Hotel – the city's largest venue – was chosen by Colonel Parker as the site for Elvis's first live shows in public since 1961.

The choice of a residency in Las Vegas, rather than a tour of the contemporary rock venues that his recent studio work might have suggested, showed again that Colonel Parker was looking far beyond the youth market. Elvis was being marketed as an international celebrity, on a par with Sinatra, Sammy Davis Jnr., Dean Martin or Barbra Streisand. The Las Vegas setting – home to mobsters and stars, and also the dream vacation for tens of millions of working Americans – brought prestige and, in Parker's eyes, class; it also had the advantage that Elvis and his massive entourage could settle in one place for four weeks at a time.

Publicity surrounding the comeback was intense, and it was vital that the performances matched the hype. Besides a full orchestra, Elvis recruited a band of top sessionmen, like James Burton, Jerry Scheff and Ronnie Tutt, plus female soul group The Sweet Inspirations and gospel combo The Imperials. Though Burton was the bandleader, Elvis himself supervised the arrangements, and the choice of material.

In true Vegas style, his repertoire featured his own hits, old and new, alongside a selection of popular standards – a nod to The Beatles with a medley of 'Yesterday' and 'Hey Jude', The Bee Gees' 'Words', Del Shannon's 'Runaway' and evergreens like the Ray Charles hit 'I Can't Stop Loving You' and Willie Nelson's 'Funny How Time Slips Away'. The combination of a rock'n'roll group, playing rockabilly licks as if it was still 1956, an orchestra and two vocal groups gave Presley's show an exhilarating impact. Though the ensemble sometimes veered into cabaret-style slickness, at their best they were thrillingly loud and raw, with the orchestra soothing the ears of those too middle-aged to rock.

The set-up in Vegas – the arrangements and even the basic repertoire – effectively determined the future course of Elvis's live career. The difference in 1969, and for the next two or three years as well, was that he sang as if he cared. Joking with the audience one minute, he could throw himself into an extended 'Suspicious Minds' the next. Though the Fifties oldies tended towards caricature, played too fast in an attempt to match the excitement of the originals, the ballads and the newer additions to the repertoire packed a giant emotional punch.

Most of that is captured on 'Elvis In Person At The International Hotel', originally issued as part of a double-album with 'Back In Memphis' in 1969, and now available separately on CD. Taped towards the end of his first four-week residency, it caught Elvis before he'd grown bored with the hits. 'I Can't Stop Loving You' rocked like an R&B classic, while the 'Mystery Train'/'Tiger Man' medley was as hot as anything from the '68 TV special. Best of all was the eight minutes of 'Suspicious Minds', with Elvis driving the band through one chorus after another as if he never wanted the moment to end. After that, the closing 'Can't Help Falling In Love' sounded like a sincere message to the world.

One of three CDs that made up the 'Collectors Gold' box added a bunch of leftovers from these 1969 shows to the canon. They included rare on-stage performances of songs like 'This Is The Story' and 'Inherit The Wind', the usual round-up of rushed rockers, a fiery medley of 'Mystery Train' and 'Tiger Man', and the infamous 'laughing' version of 'Are You Lonesome Tonight' – a three-minute descent into hysterical giggles that was a hit single in the early Eighties. Only 'The Laughing Policeman' runs it close.

ON STAGE (1970)

The initial Vegas season was a dramatic success, both financially and critically. In January 1970, Elvis was back at the International Hotel, and as usual, RCA's

recording unit weren't far behind. The second season spawned another fine live LP, conceived with the idea of introducing ten new songs to Elvis's repertoire. All of them had been recorded by other artists in the past, but Presley made Tony Joe White's swamp-rocker 'Polk Salad Annie' his own. He relished its stop-start rhythm, its deliberately exaggerated imagery, and the opportunities it gave him to demonstrate his karate routines during the instrumental breaks.

Nothing else on the 'On Stage' album burned that hot, but Elvis's renditions of Joe South's 'Walk A Mile In My Shoes', the country standard 'Release Me' and even the vintage blues song, 'See See Rider', came pretty close. There was also a hit single in the wings, in the revival of 'The Wonder Of You'. RCA made up the numbers with two songs from the first Vegas residency, 'Yesterday' (with its 'Hey Jude' ending excised) and 'Runaway'.

Available on CD in very reasonable sound quality.

ELVIS – THAT'S THE WAY IT IS (1970)

The film of this title shared some songs but no performances with the supposed 'soundtrack' album (see Section E). The movie, Presley's first documentary, was a wonderful record of the third Las Vegas engagement, in August/September 1970. It included much backstage and rehearsal footage, plenty of songs from the Vegas shows, and also some snippets from the first night of a brief nationwide tour in September.

LAS VEGAS HILTON (February 1972)

In 1971, the International Hotel became the Las Vegas Hilton. After a second tour at the end of 1970, Elvis returned to Vegas in January 1971. That July/August he tried a residency in another desert playground, at the Sahara Tahoe in Stateline, before returning to the renamed Hilton in August. November saw him on tour again; then in January 1972 he was ready for Vegas one more time.

No album came from these dates, but

ELVIS ON TOUR (1972)

The last Presley movie was another fine documentary, this time covering a series of concerts across the USA in April 1972. Despite the quality of many of the performances in the film, RCA declined to issue a soundtrack album. For some months, though, they toyed with a concept called 'Standing Room Only' – the working title for the film, as well. This LP would have followed the format of 'Elvis – That's The Way It Is', in mixing live and studio recordings. Though it would have masqueraded as a movie soundtrack, the live recordings would actually have come from the Las Vegas shows mentioned above.

ELVIS AS RECORDED AT MADISON SQUARE GARDEN (1972)

Madison Square was an event. Elvis's two shows at the Garden on June 10, 1972 were – remarkably enough – his first ever concerts in New York City. Even during the halcyon touring days of 1955-57, he'd never dared to take Manhattan. Now he did, and in style.

RCA did tape several shows. 'It's Impossible' ended up on the 1973 LP 'Elvis'; a few other songs surfaced after Presley's death; and most important of all, a stirring version of the patriotic 'An American Trilogy' appeared as a single, becoming a major hit in Britain.

The grandeur of the occasion actually stood for more than the music. RCA did their best to make the souvenir album as important as the concerts by rushing it into the stores before June was over, but the speed took its toll. Despite some worthwhile moments – a surprisingly powerful version of 'The Impossible Dream', and a thoughtful, sly take on Hoyt Axton's 'Never Been To Spain', the 'Madison Square Garden' album sounded rushed and lacklustre. And worse was to come.

Reproduced faithfully on CD.

ALOHA FROM HAWAII BY SATELLITE (1973)

Another event, another album – a double, this time. Broadcast live by satellite to every corner of the globe apart from Britain (where we had to wait years for the opportunity to see the show), and America, where it wasn't seen for another three months, this concert found Elvis in the H.I.C. Arena in Honolulu on January 14, 1973. Within a month, the album of the show was in the shops, with the predictable array of hits and standards enlivened by the recent single, 'Burning Love', a heartfelt rendition of Marty Robbins' 'You Gave Me A Mountain', and a playful slide through James Taylor's 'Steamroller Blues'. The rest was fine when accompanied by the visuals, but less exciting as a record to play at home.

After the audience had left the arena, Elvis and his band (essentially unchanged since the first Vegas shows, though with J.D. Sumner & The Stamps replacing The Imperials) stayed on, to record several Hawaiian songs which were inserted into rebroadcasts of the live show.

Available in all its dubious glory on CD.

THE ALTERNATE ALOHA (1973; issued 1988)

Two days before the live broadcast, Elvis and his entire band ran through their entire Honolulu show before an audience of 6,000 people – partly as a rehearsal, partly to give RCA something to fall back on if the live concert recordings weren't up to scratch. The rehearsal show circu-

lated on bootleg for years, and was finally made available by RCA in the late Eighties. Sadly, the disastrous mix, and the similarity to the 'Aloha From Hawaii' set, left most Elvis fans dissatisfied.
Available on CD.

ELVIS AS RECORDED LIVE ON STAGE IN MEMPHIS (1974)

This wasn't an event; this was desperation. Unbeknown to the fans, who could only wonder why RCA had decided to issue their fifth Elvis live set in as many years, Presley had elected not to enter the recording studio during 1974. With his last LP, 'Good Times', having flopped, the label fell back on the trusty standby of an in-concert record, which duly made the Top 40.

Another patchy, poorly-mixed effort, 'Live On Stage In Memphis' did shine briefly, when Elvis was joined by J.D. Sumner and The Stamps for an emotional 'How Great Thou Art'. Kris Kristofferson's 'Why Me Lord' was also featured, though the potential of the song was undercut when it became a vehicle for Sumner's below-

bass vocal theatrics. Otherwise, the only novelty in a predictable list of songs was a minute or so of the Loggins and Messina hit 'Your Mama Don't Dance' during a rock'n'roll medley.

HAVING FUN WITH ELVIS ON STAGE (1974)

The weirdest Elvis live album of all: little more than 30 minutes of song introductions and endless requests for water, prepared by Colonel Parker as a souvenir for those who loved the comedian more than the singer.
Not available on CD – and not likely to be.

THE CONCERT YEARS (1975; issued 1980)

As part of their mammoth 'Elvis Aron Presley' boxed set, RCA delved into their archives and discovered an unissued set of live recordings from June 1975. Taped in Dallas and Shreveport, they included a couple of interesting song selections – the rocker 'T-R-O-U-B-L-E' and the Fifties doo-wop novelty, 'Little Darlin' ' among the usual array of standards.

LAS VEGAS HILTON
(December 1975)

Two songs taped by a fan, and given to RCA after Elvis's death, appeared on posthumous singles. RCA were forced to use what were effectively bootleg recordings because their own staff had failed to capture rare Presley performances of 'Softly As I Leave You' and 'America The Beautiful'.

ELVIS IN CONCERT (1977)

Just two months before his death, an overweight, sometimes bewildered Elvis Presley was filmed for the last time, for a CBS TV special. If Elvis had lived, then this footage would probably have been shelved, as it revealed the depths of his physical decline. Under the circumstances, though, it was rushed through post-production, and ready for screening six weeks after the tragedy – accompanied by the tie-in album.

The record was actually a double-LP, the first the soundtrack of the TV show, the second filled with other recordings from the same concerts in Omaha and Rapid City. The soundtrack songs were mostly painful to hear – and to see, as Elvis was reduced to reading the words to 'My Way' from a piece of paper – but they included an astonishingly powerful 'How Great Thou Art'. The second album proved that Elvis was still bothering to vary his repertoire a little, with rare performances of 'Fairytale', 'And I Love You So' and 'Early Morning Rain'.

CD Compilations

Besides the collections which focus on a particular era of Elvis's career, and are listed within each of the relevant chronological sections, there are a number of CDs in the shops which attempt some kind of overview of Presley's entire output.

ELVIS — THE LEGEND (1983)

Issued as a three-CD set, on both gold and silver-coloured discs, this package has exactly the same contents as the four volumes of 'The Collection' issued a couple of years later, which are surveyed elsewhere. It's a useful selection of Elvis recordings from 1954 to 1972, but memorable mainly for being issued in a limited edition, with the result that it rapidly hit the £100 mark on the collectors' market.

RECONSIDER BABY (1985)

After years of dubious RCA concoctions, an album which focused on Elvis the blues singer was greeted with open arms. Musically, it's varied and superb, while completists will relish its alternate take of 'One Night' (cut with the original, uncensored lyrics) and its unusual mixes of several songs. The sound quality isn't everything it could have been, however, and RCA's boxed sets are gradually making CDs like this irrelevant.

A VALENTINE GIFT FOR YOU (1985)

For who? Not me, bud. Elvis sings romantically, on a selection of songs which all predate the '68 comeback.

BALLADS (1986)

'Moody Blue', 'It's Only Love' and especially 'Suspicious Minds' are too fast to qualify as ballads, while the choice of songs is both too predictable and too eclectic – achieving that ambivalent status by placing 'Hawaiian Wedding Song', of all things, alongside the expected 'Can't Help Falling In Love' and 'Wooden Heart'.

RARE ELVIS (1986)

Three vinyl albums appeared under this title, but only the first made it onto CD. Included were some non-album singles and B-sides (several of them from the early Seventies, making this a useful place to find the studio version of 'Patch It Up' and 'The First Time Ever I Saw Your Face'), several of the after-show songs from the 'Aloha From Hawaii' date in 1973, a version of the Fifties film song 'Lover Doll' without The Jordanaires, and the contents of the 1958 documentary EP, 'Elvis Sails', which chronicles Presley's departure for Army service in Germany. An interesting selection, not matched by the sound quality.

ALL TIME GREATEST HITS (1987)

Recommended both for its sound and its song selection, this is the best short-form introduction to Elvis. Across two CDs, it brings together 45 of his biggest and best singles, from 1956 ('Heartbreak Hotel') to 1977 ('Way Down'). The reproduction is far superior to the other 'hits' CDs — plus there's the bonus of rare mixes of 'Suspicious Minds' and 'Always On My Mind'.

I WISH YOU A MERRY CHRISTMAS (1987)

A mixture of tracks from the classic Fifties Christmas album, and its somewhat less classic 1971 successor.

THE LEGEND LIVES ON (1990)

A mail-order selection of hits spread across five CDs – worth buying as an introduction to the man's work, and also because it includes an alternate version of 'Easy Question' from the early Sixties, and some stereo mixes otherwise unobtainable on CD.

THE GREAT PERFORMANCES (1990)

As the first legal home for 'My Happiness', one of the songs from Elvis's first ever acetate, this CD has its place in history. But the inclusion of that track on the 'Fifties Masters' boxed set makes this haphazard selection irrelevant. Note, however, that the line-up does include 'Unchained Melody' from 1977 before it received its studio overdubs.

COLLECTOR'S GOLD (1991)

Until the release of 'The Complete Fifties Masters' and 'From Nashville To Memphis' provided welcome reassurance, this three-CD package suggested that RCA's well-intentioned archive series was running slightly off the rails. On one count, everything here matched the title – there were two CDs full of studio out-takes, one apiece from Nashville and Hollywood sessions; and another CD taken from the memorable Vegas shows of August 1969. Of these, the Vegas tapes were the most important (see Section 6 for more info); by comparison, almost all of the film and studio out-takes were little more than ephemeral.

The Hollywood tracks are listed in Section 3, film by film: the only notable offering was 'Black Star', unissued before in any form, and intended as the original theme song for what became *Flaming Star*. The Nashville studio cuts were more welcome, simply because the raw material was better. They included first-time releases for the 1963 versions of 'Ask Me' and 'Memphis, Tennessee', plus alternate takes of Sixties cuts like 'Love Letters', 'Like A Baby' and 'Witchcraft'. In themselves, there was nothing wrong with these tracks, but all the studio cuts paled alongside the Fifties out-takes included on the 'Essential Elvis' collections.